D0691391

Deep Writing

By the Same Author

Fiction

The Black Narc
The Kingston Papers
Dismay
The Blackbirds of Mulhouse
The Fretful Dancer

Nonfiction

Staying Sane in the Arts
Artists Speak
A Life in the Arts
Fearless Creating
Affirmations for Artists
Fearless Presenting

Eric Maisel

Jeremy P. Tarcher / Putnam
a member of Penguin Putnam Inc.   *New York*

7

Principles

That

Bring

Ideas

to

Life

Deep Writing

Most Tarcher/Putnam books are available at special quantity
discounts for bulk purchases for sales promotions, premiums, fund-raising,
and educational needs. Special books or book excerpts also can be created
to fit specific needs. For details, write: Putnam Special Markets,
375 Hudson Street, New York, NY 10014.

Jeremy P. Tarcher/Putnam
a member of Penguin Putnam Inc.
375 Hudson Street, New York, NY 10014
http://www.penguinputnam.com

Copyright © 1999 by Eric Maisel
All rights reserved. This book, or parts thereof,
may not be reproduced in any
form without permission.
Published simultaneously in Canada

Library of Congress Cataloging-in-Publication Data

Maisel, Eric, date.
Deep writing : seven principles that bring ideas to life /
Eric Maisel.
p.   cm.
ISBN 0-87477-947-2
1. Authorship—Psychological aspects.   2. Authors—Psychology.
3. Creation (Literary, artistic, etc.)   4. Emotions.   I. Title.
PN171.P83M35   1999
808'.02'019—dc21   98–36116 CIP

Printed in the United States of America
1   3   5   7   9   10   8   6   4   2

This book is printed on acid-free paper. ⊗

Book design by Ralph L. Fowler

Acknowledgments

First, I would like to thank all the folks at Tarcher/Putnam, a few of whom I know and most of whom I don't, who have contributed to the making of this book. My thanks especially to Jeremy Tarcher, for his continuing support and good conversation in airport restaurants, and to Wendy Hubbert, this book's editor, who has had the painful task of telling me more times than either of us can count that this or that still needed fixing.

Next, I would like to thank the writers I have seen in my creativity consulting and psychotherapy practices, and those I have visited with at workshops and writers' conferences, for their contributions to my understanding of the challenges and joys of writing. I would also like to thank the many people who have written to me, often at length, about their experiences in the arts and their thoughts and feelings about the creative life. One of those letters has an important place in this book; all of them are important to me. Thank you all.

Last, I would like to thank my family, whose love and support are valuable beyond reckoning.

For Ann, with love and gratitude

Contents

Deep Writing

Introduction

I've been counseling writers for the past fifteen years, first as a psychotherapist and now as a creativity consultant. For the past ten years I've also taught writing at the college level, to adults returning to school after a significant absence. And I've been writing for nearly thirty years—novels and self-help nonfiction, articles and short stories, for big publishing houses and miniature houses, for professional houses and commercial houses, as a ghostwriter and under my own name. From these three adventures—as writer, writing teacher, and writers' counselor—I've learned a lot.

I put many of my thoughts about creativity and the creative life in my previous books, like *Fearless Creating, A Life in the Arts,* and *Affirmations for Artists.* But although much of what I had to say in those books was of use to writers, I never set out to write a book exclusively for them, my creative brethren. Now seems like exactly the right moment. As I cross fifty, with more than twenty books under my belt, many of them published and many of them unpublished, it is a great pleasure, bordering on a thrill, to stop and chat with my fellow writers about our special calling.

What do I want to accomplish in this book? First, I'd like to help you write, if you happen to want to write. Second, I'd like to help you write deeply, if you're going to write at all. By "writing deeply" I mean: writing passionately and well about those things that really matter to you. I think that I have a good idea how people can get from not-writing to writing and from writing to writing deeply, and this is what I will share with you in the following pages. The process of becoming a deep writer involves the following seven principles:

1. Hushing the Mind
2. Holding the Intention
3. Making Choices
4. Honoring the Process
5. Befriending the Work
6. Evaluating the Work
7. Doing What's Required

As I explain these seven principles to you, I'll offer some advice about how to put them into practice, and provide some exercises to help you get started. In addition, because every writer is unique, I've invented case studies of five writers from differing backgrounds to help us explore how these principles apply to people with various needs and life experiences. Let me introduce our five fictional writers.

Amelia. Now in her late twenties, Amelia writes short stories, poetry, and social commentary. She lives her life at the chaotic end of the spectrum, and her relationships tend toward the intense, the volatile, and the dramatic. She drinks enough that she is beginning to call it a problem; she experiences occasional but severe bouts of depression; and her day job is virtually unbearable. She is a stylish, fluent writer but feels uncertain about what to write next. She would like to tackle something large and grand, but she can't put her finger on what that might be.

Marjorie. In her late forties, Marjorie is married and has college-age children. She was an English major in college; she's always wanted to write but never has. She is thinking about writing a novel—a dream and a goal she has painfully kept alive for almost thirty years. She is soft-spoken, self-critical, and critical of others, although she doesn't like to be thought of as judgmental. She has the idea that she might like to write a historical novel or maybe an adventure yarn for young adults. But she doesn't feel close to choosing a topic or beginning to write.

Sam. Sam doesn't think of himself as a writer. But for career reasons he's embarked on a doctoral program in business that requires him to produce a dissertation. Sam is in his mid-thirties, works in the computer industry, and thinks of himself primarily as a problem-solver. He doubts that his grammar and spelling are all that good, but he has faith in his computer's spell checking and grammar checking programs. What really worries him is "getting an idea" important enough to pursue and solid enough to pass the muster of his dissertation committee. Every day he falls further behind on the preparation of his dissertation proposal. When asked how the proposal is going, he replies, "It's not! I'm a terrible procrastinator!"

Anne. Anne has always written. Early in life, she thought

she'd become an archaeologist or a filmmaker, but without making any conscious choice she discovered that she'd written her first novel by the time she was twenty-two. It never got published, and neither did her second, but her third did. It sold modestly well, and subsequently Anne managed to sell three other novels. But she has had to scramble to make ends meet, working day jobs and teaching creative writing at a local college. At thirty-eight, she retains few romantic illusions about the writer's life, but she still feels passionate about writing. She wonders if now is the time to attempt a formula novel or some kind of bestseller fiction that will catapult her out of the midlist.

Henry. An urbane, bisexual playwright and screenwriter in his mid-fifties, Henry is currently in a relationship with a man but doesn't consider himself gay. Sexual identity issues have always troubled and tormented him, but he's never confronted them in his writing. Recently he was mistakenly diagnosed as HIV+ and for three months lived with that diagnosis. He has written successful light comedies for the stage and lots of script rewrites for Hollywood movies, dividing his time between New York and Los Angeles. But his reluctance to write about what really matters has begun to irritate and anger him. He wonders if now might be the time for him to write a play that examines bisexuality and, if it is, whether he should write it as a gritty drama or as a British-style comedy.

Obviously these five writers can't represent everyone. To represent us all I'd have to include an African-American poet from the South, a Latina playwright from Los Angeles, a New Age therapist tackling self-help nonfiction, an urban cowboy writing westerns, an academic writer, an octogenarian who still dreams of writing, and thousands more. But even though I can't possibly characterize all writers, I can say quickly what we have in common.

Each of us is a human being.

Each of us recapitulates human nature in a particular way.

Each of us is a product of heredity and environment.

Each of us is troubled and challenged in multiple ways.

Each of us has appetites, dreams, ambitions, doubts, anxieties, loves, prejudices, and depressions.

We are all in the same boat. We are all full of secret shames and desires, real loyalties and real disloyalties, keen self-understanding and spectacular self-idiocy. We are all capable of making every human mistake possible, and we all go ahead and make tons and tons of them.

We also all aspire to become meaning-makers. The more we want "to give a shape to our fate," as Albert Camus put it, the more the meanings we make or fail to make concern us. A meaning-maker is a person who takes her humanity and experiences and attempts to put them together coherently, artfully, beautifully, but at the very least *somehow,* for her own sake and for the sake of others. That product may or may not change the world, or even reach the world. But a meaning-maker can do nothing less than struggle to make meaning, because meaning-making is a moral imperative.

Jonathan Kozol wrote that he started out hoping to change the world but had to reframe his mission: now he considers himself a witness. His work and his moral imperative haven't changed, only his expectations. The writer is a lifelong meaning-maker, upset about something in the world, angry at some injustice, working through personal confusion and uncertainty, dismayed that others have failed to see this or that, obsessed about knowing, trying to connect, trying to speak, needing to create.

Writers make meaning, if we are inclined to do so, because of a certain self-relationship into which we've entered. I don't know why some people enter into this self-relationship and others don't, but part of it is probably constitutional. Some babies probably pop right out of the womb stubbornly disbelieving dogma and fiercely fixated on truth, beauty, and goodness. This child at four, five, and six is already self-directing, already disgusted and angered by the falseness and wishy-washiness of the normal. She may smile, comply, do the dishes, and trot off to school, but inside wheels are spinning and gears are grinding. "Now, what is really true about the world and what is just convention?" this child is wondering. "What's good and what's bad? How can I use myself, amuse myself, and do some grand things?"

These aren't direct quotes. A child doesn't use this language. But he is mesmerized by books, because of what they contain and what they can accomplish. He is entranced by music, by dance, by bugs crawling everywhere in evolutionary profusion, by tales that examine the human predicament, by the mysterious look of the sky at night. In wordless ways a connection to the task of personal meaning-making grows ever stronger in him, so that, at the age of twenty-three, he decides to live in Africa and study tigers, make documentary films that puncture the authority of church and corporation, or write Taoist-influenced poetry about silence.

I seem to be saying that this existentially inclined self-relationship is the particular birthright of only some human beings. Yet I have the equally strong feeling that pretty much everyone feels the same way, beneath all the unfortunate training that turns stubborn meaning-makers into self-estranged adults willing to accept the self-imposed exile of an uncreative life. I think that *you* are that stubborn meaning-maker, ready to write real things with your own blood, even if you've only been wishing and wishing to do so, decade after decade, without ever beginning.

Human beings are psychological creatures. This may seem self-evident, yet the writer who does not write, or who writes but does not write deeply, rarely turns to herself to ask, "What's my nature, and what in my nature is the problem?" A writer is much more inclined to take a hundred workshops than to stop and say, "My parents did a terrific job of controlling me and maybe I've turned into a control freak myself. That's a real problem! If I'm spending all my energy trying to control things, there's no chance I can write deeply."

Freud may have been wrong in six hundred and three ways, but he was right about this: we are made up of intrapsychic conflicts and a lot of other roiling stuff. Our insides really are dynamic, so much so that we can get twisted up early on and never untwist, so much so that we can obsess about the correct inner temperature for medium rare roast beef or whether Christ was born on Wednesday, Thursday, or Friday, and in the process never get our work done. We have been speculating intensely for a hundred years now about how each of us gets twisted, and how we might untwist, but—as evidenced by the inability of most of us to make lasting, important changes in our life—we have a long way yet to go.

I would like you to be a good, productive human being and

to discover lots of eloquent personal meaning. In order to do these things, you will need to scrutinize yourself. I'm afraid I'll be asking you to do exactly this. Maybe I'll end up annoying and irritating you with this particular lecture and this particular request. Maybe I've irritated you already! But most writing books are far too happy-go-lucky and undemanding and make the most absurd promises. "If you can order Chinese food, you can be Dostoevsky!" "If you can count to ten, you can get happily published!" My message is different. You can write deeply, but you will have to sweat a little.

We are also embedded in the cultural and historical realities of the country in which we are born and raised. While not everyone is sucked into the vortex of the latest trial, scandal, technology, sitcom, blockbuster movie, shopping mall opening, or Elvis Presley sighting in the same way, everyone does exist right here and right now, and there is no escape from that. In this moment, as a consequence of perfectly comprehensible evolutionary reasons, each of us is more anxious and more prone to depression than ever before in human history. Right now, more is in question, more is uncertain, and firm meanings are harder to come by. These and other contemporary curses are the fruit of this particular moment. So we will have to be mindful of this moment and mindful of the multiple challenges that come with it, because this moment really does affect whether, and how deeply, we write.

If we are mindful of the moment, we also realize that this particular publishing marketplace—the marketplace of chain bookstores and independent bookstores, audio books and nonbooks, bestseller lists and niche titles—however it operates and whatever it represents, is exactly the market in which writers must ply their wares. Only through this marketplace, as it really and truly exists, can writers bring their chunks of constructed meaning to the attention of readers. But even if a writer examines the marketplace and decides to write something commercial, she may still not guess right about what's wanted or what will be in vogue when her book is finished. She may decide to put her own spin on a genre and take the book right out of that genre. She may write a good book but not reach the right marketplace players. She may even write a good book, reach the marketplace, and still only earn from her two- or three-year adventure what a surgeon makes in an afternoon.

We have to be aware of these painful realities, and also that a particular piece of writing may not turn out well. It is entirely possible to spend a year or two writing deeply, working every day with attention and integrity, and still end up producing a book that misses the mark. Maybe it's wonderful in some parts but badly flawed in others. Maybe you tried to solve a riddle that is presently insoluble. Maybe you chose the wrong structure, the wrong voice, the wrong angle. Any of this can happen. All of this *does* happen.

Many failed works—works moldering in drawers, works that never were and never will be published—are the fruits of deep writing. For instance, I spent all of 1996 writing a book called *Lighting the Way,* for which I received the first half of an advance of twenty-five thousand dollars. It was a book in which I tried to say some important things about the brain, human nature, and the contours of the present moment. In the course of writing it I began to articulate a philosophy of life I called vitalism, a philosophy tangentially based on the ancient philosophy of the same name with roots dating back to Aristotle and a checkered history in biology.

But the book didn't work. Neither the editor-in-chief nor the publisher who had paid the first half of the advance could support it or imagine publishing it. I really didn't know that the book didn't work, although I did have some doubts about it all along. But after the publishing house rejected it and time passed, I reread it and saw that the book was so flawed that only a collector of cracked objects could prize it. It made no difference that I'd worked on twenty books before in my life. It made no difference that I'd carefully reread and revised each chapter. The book was wrong.

All the deep writer can do is honestly chew on something. All she can ask of herself is honest effort and right intention. Deep writing arises from this effort to really wrestle with something, to honorably and truthfully make sense of something, making use of the known and acknowledging, as best as one's defenses permit, all that is not known. If a writer does that, sometimes miracles will happen. One may end up with, as Freud said of Dostoevsky's *The Brothers Karamazov,* a "perfectly motivated" novel, or a brilliant, beautiful, truthful nonfiction book. Even if the work is genre work or work for hire, if the writer determines first of all to chew on something, on a truth about human nature, on a moral dilemma, on something worthy and grand, sometimes a great piece of deep writing will emerge.

You might call deep writing engaged writing. What is it that is engaged? Your whole being. You bring everything that you are, your brain, your heart, your experiences, your loves and hates, your trace memories and this morning's news, to a certain quiet state of readiness; you empty your mind, activate your mind, and write as if entranced. You are engaged, as lovers are engaged, and as existentialists use the word. The wind stops whistling. The clock stops ticking. The universe stops for the sake of your deep writing.

Deep writing is work meant *to mean* and not just entertain, garner applause, or demonstrate one's skills. *Hiroshima, 1984, On the Beach, Crime and Punishment, The Trial, The Mayor of Casterbridge, The Death of the Heart, The Stranger,* the novels of Sigrid Undset, James Baldwin's *Giovanni's Room,* Simenon's psychological thrillers are a few of the novels I read in my youth that I believe were intended to be about something. Each writer had a dream, a problem to solve, a truth to tell, a moral imperative, a holy quest, all mixed up together.

I haven't yet called deep writing spiritual work. I'm rather loath to do so now. First of all, I have no idea what "spiritual" means. I see deep writing as supremely human work, maybe *the* human work, and to call it spiritual adds nothing to its importance from my point of view. But there is an important "but." I do believe that who we are, why we're here, and what the universe is all about are utter mysteries, mysteries that science can't unravel and theology fears. If "spiritual" means something like living this mystery—living in relation to this mystery and in awareness of this mystery—rather than living ordinarily, then I feel more comfortable calling deep writing spiritual work. In fact, I'm happy to call it that. I'm happy to agree with Goethe when he said, "Existence is God." In this sense, as workers in the mystery, deep writers form part of the spiritual core of society. They are human, but because they focus on the mystery of humanity they are also our spiritual leaders.

I've been writing this book afternoons. Mornings I work on a book about creativity and psychology that's geared for therapists and their clients. Today I wrote about a poet, a woman I saw in therapy a dozen years ago, whose mind housed every inner demon imaginable. To recollect her is to remember how burdened each person is by his or her psychological nature. Because of this profound fact, we'll focus first on the subject of inner demons—of personality and psychological structure.

Our psychological "issues" really do prevent us from holding ideas, starting on projects, maintaining momentum, and respecting ourselves and our efforts. We need to get well, or at least better, because we deserve relief from pain and we need emotional freedom. As the poet I just mentioned expressed it, "When I am completely healthy, completely healed, will there be more art in me? I think there will be and maybe it will be some of the best. That sense of wholeness and well-being must be a wonderful place to make art from. I hope I get a chance to be there, even if only for a while."

Let's begin, then, with a look at the mind of the writer.

Hushing
the
Mind

We bring our personality with us when we write (or fail to write). This is a fact, and for some of us a tragedy. Life is short and hard enough that it would be nice if we were allowed by the muse to glide to the computer free of doubts and inner demons. But like cement blocks around our ankles these anxieties pull us down, these personality parts that we never asked for and can hardly comprehend. They pull us down past the depths where we would willingly swim, down to the ocean floor where light cannot penetrate.

This is an ominous beginning to an optimistic chapter. But the facts speak for themselves. Writers have a hard time of it because we all have a hard time of it. I know more intelligent people than I can count who want to write and have it in them to write but who either do not write deeply or do not write at all.

Why? Not because writing is hard. Yes, it is hard, but it is also as easy as dreaming or thinking, both of which the brain is built to do. It is this ease that eludes all these intelligent people. Why? Because they are stymied by their own personalities.

If there were nothing to be done about this, it would be unkind to mention it. But I've had the experience hundreds of times over of helping people begin to write or begin to write more deeply. The secret is simple: Learn to manage your mind. If I can get you to manage your mind, I will have gotten you to do an enormous thing—I will have gotten you to "change" and "improve" your personality. Consider the Buddha's metaphor: "This mind of mine went formerly about as it liked, as it listed, as it pleased; but I shall now hold it firmly, as the rider who wields the hook holds in the furious elephant." So get a grip. Get a grip on your own mind.

Personality resides in every pore of our being, but it presents itself for review in the mind. Only it presents itself in whispers. There's the rub! You can hear these whispers, since they are meant to affect and influence you, but at the same time they are elusive and slippery. So you must listen attentively for what you can barely hear and do not really want to hear, the words of these inner demons scolding, insulting, and mocking you. Then, having heard them clearly for the first time, you must silence them. Silence!

A new client came to see me recently. He was a Phi Beta Kappa from an Ivy League college, had been the managing editor of a major magazine, and had just signed his first book contract. He wondered if he would be able to write his book at the pace of a page or two a day. Every devil in the underworld was laughing. What could prevent this man from writing a few hundred words a day on a topic he'd been thinking about and studying for twenty years? What else could it be except his own history, his own personality?

We are not mad, most of us, but our minds nevertheless resemble lunatic asylums. It is real bedlam in there. This is what cognitive therapists have been telling us for several decades and analysts for a century. No, when you are watching television or pruning the roses, all hell is not breaking loose in your mind. Then a passive quiet obtains. The asylum is quiet, drugged, dreamy, asleep. But as soon as you say "Shall I write?" all hell breaks loose. The demons arise, shrieking. Then it is bedlam. Why? Because at that moment, at the very moment when you would like to take yourself seriously and come alive, just as you stand up to speak, the furious elephants the Buddha identified are trained to unleash themselves. Just as you would like to stand up and speak, your own personality says, sit down, shut up!

Our demons shriek, "How dare you! Impossible! That you would even think of writing!" Or do they whisper? My sense is that these demons have their own peculiar sound, or no sound, like voices in dreams. We get the message without the sound waves; we see lips moving but no vocal cords vibrate. This makes it all very devilish! Because we are our own personality wrapped into, around, and through ourselves, we talk—chastise, berate, insult—ourselves perfectly telepathically. Whole conversations pass out of earshot and we are left with a boulder on the chest, crushing us, or a spear in the heart, killing possibilities. How dramatic! But these are the dramas that honestly go on. These are the dramas that cheat us and keep us from creating.

Hushing the mind, the principle of this chapter, means first of all silencing the demons that destroy our resolve and drown out our good ideas. Silencing them how? The analyst says, go back to childhood and start there. Lie down. Don't look at me. Begin. The supportive therapist says, talk to me, tell me your troubles, we can work this out together. The cognitive therapist says, let's eavesdrop on these conversations and see what's being said. Whenever you hear something you don't like, say something different. The narrative therapist says, you've been living a made-up story of your life, a fiction, and we'll make up a different story together, a better fiction.

Bizarrely enough, the solution is simpler than these therapeutic answers. All you have to do is say "hush" and mean it. You don't even have to say the word, since this work is internal and telepathic. All you have to do is just *mean* "hush" and *become* a living silence. Too simple? Not hardly. Just try becoming a living silence!

A letter to the editor at *Writer's Digest* once chastised me for the advice I'd given in that magazine on hushing. The letter said, "I've been subjected to mountains of psychobabble and psycho mumbojumbo, but never—never—anything approaching the unending stream of inanities in 'Nurturing the Wish to Create' by Eric Maisel. With all due respect, can Maisel's stuff be real?"

I understand this writer's anger and disbelief. But what I wrote was, and continues to be, true. All I can do is explain myself further. There is bedlam inside our own minds, and we must quiet it. The best way to quiet it is also the simplest: to just say "S-s-s-sh." It is exactly what the good parent does for the unhappy child when she whispers, "Hush little baby, don't you cry."

In my creativity consulting practice, which is a hybrid of

therapy and supportive coaching, I virtually never say to the frustrated writer wanting to write, "Let's explore what happened to you when you were five or six." What I do is smile and say, "Shh." I smile and say, "Stop it." The goal is that we laugh together at the absurdity of the situation: an alive person, bursting to speak, silenced by invisible demons residing in his own skull. Shouldn't the sky weep and crack at such absurdity?

I am inclined to just say, "Hush," and often I do just say, "Hush." "Hush. Write a little." A client will frame the book that has been eluding him for the past month, year, or lifetime in the next ten minutes. In my all-day workshops I do something very similar. I say a few things, but what I am communicating is "Hush." My goal is to quiet the nerves and minds of the participants, to let the anxiety be normalized, embraced, dissipated, to silence the demons by naming them and then smiling. The results are remarkable. People write. They write and write. They write as they have wanted to write. All I provide is a path to right silence.

It isn't that I haven't the patience to hear a writer's reasons for not writing or not writing deeply. It's just that we do better in the present, hushing here, being here. If you are not writing here and now, that means that here and now demons are silencing you. To ask how they happened to inhabit your body thirty years ago is like asking how you contracted a chronic disease. That might be important to know if we didn't have the cure already. But we have the cure! We can eliminate the demons right now.

Just by hushing.

This is not esoteric knowledge or an esoteric practice. I was once invited to talk to some high school students in a creative writing class, and I presented a pair of ideas: hushing and "holding" (the subject of chapter 2). A student in the class had a question. "I know that place of quiet exactly," she said. "I just don't know how to go there often enough. How can I go there more often?"

That is the deep writer's central question. But it is not an esoteric query, like "What is soul?" or "Who made the universe?" It is just a human question, a human-sized question, a question about biology and psychology and aliveness and other natural matters. The answer to "How can I hush my mind so that I can write deeply?" is "By wanting to, by meaning to, and by practicing silence."

Hushing as Idea and Practice

Hushing the mind is a robust idea and a rich practice. As an idea, it means more than just silencing demons. It means the following:

- Engaging the mind, as gears must be engaged before a car trip can begin
- Orienting the mind toward thought
- Repaving the brain's highways to remove ruts that force our thinking down habitual paths
- Getting a grip
- Loosening our grip, as one must loosen one's grip to deliver a baby

Hushing the mind means engaging and orienting the mind as well as quieting it. What one is hushing is the noise of a busy brain doing second-class work. It's like telling panicked passen-

gers on a sinking ship, "Shut up! We have to think!" For the
brain will do second-class work unless it is ordered or invited to
do first-class work. Why? Why won't it do first-class work auto-
matically? For the same reason that you and I take the elevator
and not the stairs. For the ease of it.

This is not to disparage the mind. The mind is quite spectacular. Even in these advanced times our metaphors for mind
remain puny: to call the mind a computer or central processing
unit is to insult the mind and glorify the machine. The mind is
spectacular. It is built not to process information but to envi-
sion the shape and survival of the universe. But it is also built
to take the elevator! This is a nasty paradox that absurdist play-
wrights spend whole pages on in their journals. How can it be?
How can a fine mind happily do next to nothing? How can it
be at once so serious and so silly an organ?

It just is. It is spectacular but also lazy.

Thinking, it turns out, is simply not so popular. As one
newspaper headline put it, "No signs of intelligent life on the
New York Times bestseller list." It is not just our neighbors who
are disinclined to think; it is you and me. Few people make time
in the day to think. Few people make a cup of tea, sit down, and
say, "All right, now I'm going to frame, mull over, research, and
solve a great riddle." But I'd wager that the few who do, if they
are writers, write deeply.

Some might call this general avoidance of thinking—dis-
played by most people most of the time—a lack of curiosity. It
is common enough to say that creative people are curious while
ordinary people are not. But deep writing has little to do with
curiosity. A cat is curious. A bear is curious. A baby is curious.
But an adult human being, with hundreds of billions of

neurons ready to make worlds, is neither curious nor incurious. Such words are too mild! A writer is either alive in a first-class way or alive in a second-class way. She either pursues scientific puzzles whose lack of solution makes grown scientists weep, or she doesn't. She either writes her epic retelling of a small-town tragedy, or she doesn't. She is either in right relationship with her own mind, or she isn't.

The intelligent, sensitive person who has it in his heart to write deeply must learn that right silence and right mind are not givens. It would be nice if they were. It would be nice if you grew up in an environment that so seamlessly supported your right to think that you became an everyday deep thinker without any effort. If you've had such luck, get down on your knees in thanks! But if you haven't, you've got work to do. Who else will do it for you? Who will even encourage you? You must encourage yourself and do the simple, hard work of hushing.

We show our respect for our own mind by quieting it, by engaging it, by orienting it. We provide it with favorable conditions. We say, "I am thinking." If you do not say to yourself, "I mean to think," your mind will go about its second-class business, producing worries, opinions, and other equivalents of nothing. The mind will keep itself busy, one way or the other, because, like the heart or the lungs, it is built never to sleep. Its mandate is to never go off-line, even while its host is snoring. If the brain stops, it is time for Code Blue. So it does something all the time, this silly, splendid brain, making pointless dreams or interesting dreams, punning, calculating its bank balance, or quieting itself in preparation for master work.

A first step on the road to right silence is a repaving of the brain's neuronal highways. Hushing is like smoothing or resurfacing a road so that thoughts can arrive at their destination. Too often our thoughts get locked into habitual patterns that we repeat endlessly. We run in the same grooves, run off the road at the same spot, and end up in the same ditch. Smash! You try to think about your book, the thought travels along, grooved and locked, and, splat, it's directed back into that same damned ditch!

We repeat ourselves. The mind perseverates. The road is rutted and grooved, and beside the road are familiar ditches. The changes we want to make have to do with resurfacing that road. What I really mean, of course, is something about brain biology: that we want to help new neuronal gestalts form out of the neuronal cloud. That part of the brain that is free to make suggestions says to that part of the brain mired in habit, "Disconnect synapses, we are joining together in new ways!"

By the same token, managing the mind is both a loosening and a tightening of one's grip. But you don't need a set of complicated instructions to know when to loosen and when to tighten or how to do both at once. The principle is simple. Orient toward thought, engage your brain, let old habits of thought slip away, silence any demons that have the temerity to howl, say "Hush" and mean it. You will then experience both qualities simultaneously, the tightening and the loosening, as if a bowstring were pulled taut and an arrow let fly all in the same instant. What is that famous "Aha!"—the sound of an idea arriving—except the sound of an arrow let loose and flying? "Aha!" is the exhalation we make when we have gotten a grip and loosened that grip simultaneously. We did not have to go to archery school to learn a method. All that is required is right silence, right mind, right attention.

Let me not forget to mention the joy involved. This hushing is a really exuberant thing. It's like throwing your window open and crying, "Enough of this stale air!" Hushing the mind has something of the glorious, joyful exuberance of spring about it, as one lets one's winter thoughts escape on a gentle breeze. All winter one fretted and obsessed about the cold. All winter one had to listen to the demons trapped inside. All winter one's thoughts went down those same old grooves. But now the first buds are out! The sun is warming the world. The silence that descends is a pregnant silence filled with the sounds of swollen streams and the songs of birds. This hushing the mind, when all is said and done, is a joyful act, full of expectation and love.

Our Five Writers Grow Quiet

Let's visit with our fictitious writers: Amelia, Marjorie, Sam, Anne, and Henry.

Each has chosen to read this book, although each is (rightly) skeptical about finding answers in a book. They've just read my remarks on hushing and have different reactions. Amelia likes the idea but doubts that she is equal to the task, given her chaotic insides. Marjorie is frightened of what right silence might bring. Sam laughs at the idea of hushing and wonders why this book wasn't shelved in the New Age section of the bookstore, where he would have happily missed it. Anne understands the concept and agrees with its value, but wonders how what I'm saying is different from what she's always done. Henry, like Sam, has a negative reaction to what I'm describing, but, like Anne, he also understands the idea and accepts that a certain kind of inner silence is a prerequisite for writing. Like Anne, he just doesn't see how this hushing business is any different from what he usually does. But despite their doubts, each tries the following brief exercise.

Hushing Exercise

Find a quiet place. If there is no quiet place in your environment, that's the first thing to change.

Hear what there is to hear. Even in a quiet place, there will be sounds. You might hear the electric heater, the clock, traffic outside, the roar of an occasional bus, a computer buzz, the purring of the cat. Listen, and begin to sense how sound and silence are not incompatible. All these sounds, even the jarring ones, do not have to provoke any inner noise.

Let these sounds vanish as you turn inward. Inhale, hold the breath, begin to exhale, and softly say, "Hush." Extend the word until it becomes a long "s-s-sh," a full exhalation, a release. Let the sound trail away and your mind empty completely. Feel the good, deep darkness of inner silence.

Thoughts will come, but hush them away. Hush your thoughts until you are empty and breathing. Don't despair if you can't do this easily. Don't think about how it is not working. Just hush and hush again.

Make the exhalation very long. "Hush-sh-sh-sh-sh-sh-sh-sh-sh."

When you've done this for a while, murmur to yourself, "Deeper." Breathe deeply and fully. In a corner of your mind, perhaps in the top right portion of that silence, frame the invitation, "I am ready to write deeply." Communicate telepathically, gently, with wordless language.

Hold the complete silence that follows the invitation. If thoughts arise that are like demons or distractions, start over. If thoughts go down their old grooves, start over. If you don't feel engagement at the cellular level and an orientation toward all of humanity, start over. Let that silence fill with an imminent future of deep writing. If it fills with anything else, start over.

When, after as many tries as it takes, you've achieved right silence, go quietly, even with your eyes shut, to where you mean to write, and begin to write deeply.

Each of our writers tries this exercise and has a strong reaction.

Amelia finds that trying to hush her mind puts her into something of a frenzy. Instead of getting the quiet she wants, she gets in closer contact with her inner demons. She is reminded of her childhood in ways that she hates, reminded of the things done to her. She is reminded of her adulthood in ways she also hates, reminded of her own failures, mistakes, and disappointments. This "right silence" is all wrong! Amelia's attempts at hushing lead to a bad-feeling mania that sends her out the door in search of an adventure. Tonight she will sleep with someone in a violent, intense, altogether dramatic way.

Marjorie, although putatively in love with silence, actually doesn't like it that much, not when it's a silence meant to provoke her mind to work. She loves the silence of gardening and the silence of reading, the silence of baking and the silence of music. She even likes meditating, but she prefers physical practices like yoga and tai chi. Exercises meant to lead her to thought lead her to depression instead. She tries this exercise, but instead of hushing her mind she finds herself in bed, in real psychological pain.

Sam doesn't get it. The phrase "hushing the mind" makes him laugh. He considers himself an extrovert, a problem-solver, a realist. He's never owned a crystal or a Tarot deck or even many books. Not only doesn't he think of himself as creative, he might even be insulted if you called him that. You just might be implying that he wasn't manly or in his right mind. "Hushing the mind," he supposes, is for women and poets. He is the very opposite of Jude the Obscure, who longed for a great university but could not get there. Sam has gotten to a good university, but without any longing. There may be a spark in him somewhere, but no fire is ignited by the thought of "hushing the mind." So he drops the notion into the wastebasket, returning to his everyday business of not writing his dissertation.

Anne knows this process of hushing the mind. She does it all the time. She has quieted her mind in the service of her writing for hours on end. She knows what it feels like to invite in ideas and images; to connect observations, opinions, thoughts, and feelings out of conscious awareness into characterizations and plot; to hold a silence as vast as the universe for the sake of the birth and growth of her writing. And yet, while this is true, she wonders if she's really been all that silent recently. Hasn't deep silence been eluding her, that rich silence out of which the idea might arise for a book that will help her career? She has the unsettling feeling that her silences have gotten noisier over time, but as she tries to think about how she might change this, she discovers that she can't get quiet enough to concentrate on the question.

Henry, too, knows this silence, but he's found his own ways of keeping it at arm's length. He understands that right silence is a necessity, but he also knows that a quiet mind is a dangerous mind. Unwanted thoughts might filter up. He's like a fire walker who knows to move across the coals darn quickly. Henry creates just enough silence to write on the run. Sometimes he hushes his mind by accident, when he's having a cup of coffee or when, at dusk, he notices the silhouette of trees against a blue-black sky. In those moments, ideas announce themselves. But he hurries past those moments. He goes directly to the whiskey bottle and retrieves his busy mind, getting it back from the dangerous quiet place where it wandered for a moment.

In short, each of our five writers does not find this hushing all that easy to accomplish. Even the practiced writers, Anne and Henry, are themselves not so very practiced at hushing. Henry has reasons to avoid learning this skill, for he is trying to hide things from himself, and Anne, who is more honest, is still human enough, anxious enough, distracted enough, and in enough pain to find right silence elusive.

Each, even Sam, after he spends another week not working on his dissertation, realizes that there is work to be done in this area. Each begins to see that meeting and silencing inner demons may be an appropriate metaphor for that work. So each determines to tackle the central exercise of this chapter, called the Bedlam Walk.

The Bedlam Walk

We can't fully participate in the mystery of life if, as soon as we approach the depths where ideas reside, our own anxiety, negativity, and self-doubt make breathing difficult. If the depths unnerve us, we'll search for answers in safe places, where the air is plentiful and the sun scares demons away. But the answers we seek can't be found in those sun-drenched places. We really must dive.

We're unused to diving and afraid of diving. Intense thinking, like intense living, unnerves us. Therefore, we create categories—"geniuses" and ourselves, "real writers" and ourselves, "artists" and ourselves—and let our brain off the hook. Every would-be writer is a real writer with a head full of inner demons that prevent him or her from diving.

To say that these are not literal demons but "only" anxiety and negative self-talk is to misunderstand the drama of the situation. These, our own fears and doubts, cause the wildest inner dramas and perpetrate on us the greatest inner crimes. They really do come from hell, and they really do possess what one can't help but call aliveness. They are alive, they are demons, and they reside in that most private sanctuary of all, one's own mind.

I mentioned earlier how therapists characterize these demons. The analyst says, these demons were born in childhood. The behaviorist says, don't tell me your history, just tell me what exorcism you mean to perform. The existentialist says, your very freedom depends on the decision you make—to fight for right relationship with your own mind or to keep on running. All these views are right.

These demons infiltrated your mind a long time ago. They must be exorcised now, and you are the one who must do it. But how can you look into your own mind if that inquiry makes you break out in a sweat? Here's the answer: you meet your inner demons while also holding them at bay. You look them in the eye but without risk, and only when the time is right do you decide which demons to embrace and which to exorcise. The budding deep writer begins by meeting his inner demons in a safe, guarded way.

Imagine a room in an insane asylum. It is a harshly lit room with fifteen beds on each side and an aisle running down the middle. Each bed is occupied by a madman or a madwoman. Some of the inmates are only children. Some are hags, some homeless men, some witches. Some look entirely presentable in their business suits and sports clothes. One or two are chubby and Dickensian: smiling, kite-flying psychotics. Several look seriously normal. These are the worst!

At the far end of the room is a door, and beyond the door is a courtyard. Beyond the courtyard is a beautiful study. The study is its own self-contained building, a one-room lodge with tall windows and sunlight streaming in. Inside is a fireplace, a Persian rug, and lots of gleaming wood. Picture it however you like, but do picture it. This is your ideal study, a place where adventures of the mind can be played out from beginning to end without interruption. It is a place where fantastic questions get asked and answered. Here you write books. Here you smile that dreamy smile that plays on a writer's lips when a fine sentence gets moving, turns this way and that, and comes to a happy end.

Here you can write.

However, to get to that study you must walk down the aisle

of that asylum. You must walk through bedlam. The demons are shouting and screaming at you. No matter. Just walk down the aisle. They can't harm you. They can't pounce. They can't get off their beds. They are shrieking, impotent bastards! Yes, their words hurt. But their words are also meaningless. Since you aren't stopping to investigate their charges, you might just as well consider them false. Why not consider them false rather than true? Why not laugh and cry out, "I'm none of those things!"

Here is what they're saying, and here you are managing to walk right past them.

No-talent fool!	Stupid, incompetent dodo!
Worthless piece of snot!	Dumbass!
Weakling!	Know-nothing!
Greatest living writer—ha!	Fraud!
Spineless doormat!	Cockroach!
Total emotional mess!	Real writer's caddy!
Shithead!	Empty-headed idiot!
Absolute, utter failure!	Ridiculous impostor!
Complete illiterate!	Monster!
Intellectual midget!	Zero! Nada! Rien!

Just walk down the aisle. It doesn't matter how you get from one end to the other. No way is more heroic or more humiliating than the next. It doesn't matter if you have to crawl on your hands and knees or whistle a tune to drown out the screaming. All that matters is that you do not let these demons, who can't get off their beds and attack you, who can only rant and rave, stop you from writing. Yes, they'll make some wild leaps at you!

Yes, they'll curdle your blood with their shrieking! Just practice your hushing and keep on walking.

Open the door and leave the asylum. Isn't the courtyard's silence amazing? This is sacred silence! Enter your study. Go to the desk. Boot up the computer. If a demon's voice intrudes, say to yourself, "You're locked away, back in the asylum!" Hush and affirm that demons have no place in your study. Orient toward your work. Engage your mind. Thrive in this right silence.

Practice this exercise until you can enter right silence at will.

All right. Once you've survived your bedlam walk several times, we'll assume that you can get through hell at will. Maybe you had to do it crawling on your hands and knees. Maybe you sprinted. But however you managed it, congratulations! Now you know how to get to your study no matter what roadblocks your inner demons are erecting.

But here's a secret: the lodge has a second door. The more you become a deep writer, the less you have to fight for right silence by marching down the aisle of an insane asylum. You just move from whatever it is you're doing and undramatically enter your study by the second door. Nothing internal stands in the way. You just move from not-writing to writing.

When I present this exercise at workshops, people express how much they appreciate that second door. Yes, they could survive repeated marches through the asylum; they could take that route if they had to. But what an effort that entails! The effort is so great that most people block. Those who manage to write are forced to do so with their fingers in their ears. The bedlam still affects their work. But if you practice hushing, you can enter your writing world by that second door: it shuts tight and locks your inner demons out.

I've known writers to say, "I need all those demons with me in the study. They are my unconscious fuel, my neurotic material, my very soul." Don't you worry about that. As if any of us get fully free of our demons! One bestselling romance writer plagiarizes material from another bestselling romance writer. The most famous writer of his time, Tolstoi, as unsettled in his eighties as he was in his forties, runs away from home to die in a railway station. A well-known novelist calls me up for an appointment but fails to show up because, drunk as usual, she's fallen down a flight of steps and broken her hip. Should we worry that we might become too sane? That's hard to imagine!

When you *leave* the study—and this is very important— you can exit by either door. You can exit by the second door and bring right silence back with you, or you can exit by the first door, travel back through the asylum, and return to self-criticism and anxiety. The reasonable choice is to exit by the second door. You can return to bedlam, or you can maintain a right silence as you do the dishes, work your day job, or visit with your lover. This right silence is available to you around the clock, but achieving it takes additional practice and an additional commitment.

An Active, Hushed Mind

Silence is the theme of this chapter. You achieve silence by saying to yourself, "Hush, little baby, let us write." You say, "Move over, idiot personality, I have good work to do." You simply say, "S-s-sh."

You can begin by hushing, by orienting toward your work, or by engaging your mind. You can begin anywhere you like. Whatever you do in support of one of these objectives will support the others. When you orient toward thought, you silence demons. When you engage your mind, you get a grip. When you hush, you loosen the hold of your worries. Imagine trying to describe in words the control and surrender that go into a ballerina's series of pirouettes. Let "hush" stand for the sound of a mind so still and ready that in its pregnant space pirouettes of thought are born.

If you've played computer solitaire, you know the moment when the game's won, when you've made all the right moves and the cards are about to fly off their lines and onto their stacks. All you have to do is sit back and watch them fly. How simple and satisfying! And thinking is just like that. All sorts of preliminary work must be done, but then everything comes together in a thrilling way, the cards flying exactly where they belong, the idea arising as if by itself.

For the solitaire player this is an ecstatic moment, even though all that is occurring is the machine operating according to its program, the game being played out according to some simple rules. Yet it's exhilarating to watch the cards fly across the screen. The same thrill comes to the thinker who, having done her preliminary work—having read books, watched people in cafes, spun fantasies, peered under microscopes, taken note, and gotten quiet—all of a sudden has nothing more to do. Her brain takes over, following its own simple rules. The image of a novel-to-be or a refinement on the theory of evolution spontaneously is born.

The pieces fall into place in an active, hushed mind. You take a deep breath, stilling the universe. Then you take a voluptuous gulp of the mystery residing in that silence. From that gulp you make a world.

Holding

the

Intention

Intention is an action word. You're not really intending to do any deep writing unless and until you begin to take action. The action may "only" involve thinking or some other neuronal activity, but still there must be physical action involved, a moving of electrical current, a mixing of chemicals. If you're really intending to write, then inside your head some hammering and sawing must begin.

The deep writer holds the intention to write, which means that she acts in support of her deep writing. She might say, "I don't really do anything, I just go about my business and ideas come to me," and we are fooled by this way of talking into thinking that she's not intending anything or doing anything. But note the dreamy look on her face, the way she peers inward and listens to her own thoughts. Because she's motivated, she actively makes room in her mind for thoughts to rest awhile, she lets characters visit, she orients herself toward life's complexity and not away from it.

Motivation. Intention. Action. "Holding the intention" is a phrase meant to capture the connectedness of this writer's trinity. The deep writer has reasons to write, intends to write, and aims himself in the right direction. When you hold the intention to write you are, if not deeply writing, deeply prewriting. You have turned yourself in the direction of the sun and are prepared to worship. You have oriented yourself toward the corner of the room where your computer lives. You have your nets out to catch ideas and your tools out to build a mighty theme.

If you're holding the intention to write, that means that you're motivated. In order to sit down to write, you need reasons to write, reasons that matter to you. Otherwise why would you struggle with a blank computer screen for hours or with a novel for years? But not all motivations are of the same sort. If a deadline's nearing and you have a paper to finish, panic may motivate you. Your parents may have said something to you thirty years ago that motivates you even now: you may still be trying to prove them right or wrong. But the best motivation, the one the deep writer strives to locate and nurture, is the felt need to wrestle with ideas and emotions, with the worlds of abstract thought and intense personal feelings. This passionate wrestling is for the writer's own sake—as part of her personal meaning-making—and for the world's sake, to provide it with meaning.

The deep writer is motivated to provide the world with meaning and even to impose meaning on the world. Are you motivated this way? Are you this grandiose? Say that you are!

Stake your claim to the title of philosopher, teacher, artist, world leader.

Gripped by Ideas and Ready for Action

The idea (or theme, meaning thread, image, or vision) that the deep writer wrestles with is not a casual something in his life, not something of mere interest or importance, but a matter central to his existence and purpose on earth. Gripped by this something, he cries out, "I must explore this matter!" Coming out of a deep reverie, he exclaims, "Quick, where is my pen?" Agitated, on edge, but also excited and heartened, he whispers, "I must know whatever-this-is through writing!"

Usually it is a "whatever-this-is." It may have resonance and great depth but still be murky and inexpressible. Only rarely are writers able to put these ideas into words. Only rarely can they articulate their themes in simple sentences. The idea is understandable to the self, but no words come attached. The writer has everything she needs—a feeling in the belly, an image in the mind, some stray phrases—and she is ready to work. But as to what she is working on, she is not prepared to say. Nor does she feel compelled to articulate the idea that has suddenly arisen. All she wants to do is run to the computer and write. The theme may remain unnamed from beginning to end, until it is time to describe the work to others.

However, the fact that a deep writer can go about her business, writing a book without ever naming her idea, can prove a real problem. She can lose her place, chase a shadow, or strike off in the wrong direction. She can lose motivation, lose interest, or lose her way. In my experience, beginning writers and seasoned writers alike often do not take the time to articulate the idea for their current book in a simple sentence or two, even after the time when those few sentences could be articulated. This is a shame, because "headline" sentences of this sort can serve as a reminder, an anchor, even an affirmation throughout the writing process.

You might say, "To get the theme or idea of my book down in a simple sentence will kill it. It would lock it in place, stultify it, hamstring it. Besides, how could any single sentence do my idea justice? As if this rich thing could be said simply! Any sentence would have to be a distortion, a simplification, a travesty. Such a sentence would do me more harm than good!" My response is, I understand. I have had all of these feelings myself, many times over, and I have them to this day. Nonetheless, articulating your theme or idea in a sentence or two is a worthwhile suggestion, something to consider. To be able to do so may help you hold the intention to write and maintain motivation as you create.

For the sake of our work together, I'd like you to try naming your themes and ideas. It will be great practice. If you can point to a list on the wall and say, "These themes matter to me," you are never very far from your next deep writing project. If you can point to a single sentence that adequately, if not perfectly, captures the idea you are currently working on, you will have a constant reminder. "I want to portray a good man to see if even a good man can survive temptation." "I want to write a book for girls that helps them see that they can run great corporations and change them for the better." A useful headline like these may do only limited justice to your work, but it does the important job of reminding you of your theme and intention.

In my own life, I've spent years on novels and books of non-fiction pursuing the sorts of themes that follow, some of which I could articulate as I began writing and some of which only came clear well after the writing was under way. But *once* I could articulate the theme, however roughly and inadequately, I possessed a powerful reminder of the book's purpose and intention.

- "All mythologizing, jargonizing, and intellectualizing aside, what is the creative process really like?"
- "Isn't the only safe homeland for the Jews one far from the Middle East? Isn't Israel's very location corrupting and insane? Then why not move Israel? But where would it go, who would do the moving, and what forces would rise up to block the move?"
- "I know that many Christians envy Jews, but what exactly do they envy? Where does the envy come from? How does it grow so powerful that it leads to murder and mass murder?"
- "How can atheism be reframed as a spiritual practice?"
- "How would a quixotic, saintly modern Don Quixote live? What windmills would he joust with and what would his life look like?"
- "Why would a teacher have an affair with one of his students and ruin himself? Is appetite everything? Is appetite the only thing?"

That you have a theme or idea is vital; that you can articulate it is secondary. The starting point is more often a half-seen thing, a fleeting image, a bit of an idea. It is no sin and no problem if you commence your deep writing and proceed with your deep writing without articulating what exactly it is that you are writing. Maybe you'll come up with that neat sentence three months from now, or maybe you'll still be struggling to describe the book as you start doing interviews in support of it. But practicing this articulation process is really very important.

Some Helpful "TIPS"

To work on finding and articulating your themes and launching into your next deep writing project, try the following exercise. TIPS stands for:

- Themes
- Intention
- Plan
- Steps

If you take the time to look for them and have the courage to stare them in the eye, you will discover, barely out of conscious awareness but eager to gain your attention, a host of resonant life themes. When you think about any one of them, you immediately feel alive. But you also feel a little queasy, a little anxious. Because these themes are of the utmost importance, because the very meaning of your existence is bound up with them, they excite your mind and grip your heart.

They also signal danger. What if you discover, as you wrestle with the idea of "a good man tempted," that the fellow you're imagining, once you give him life and let him live, fails the test you've posed for him? Possibly you suspected that he would, but now you've proven it conclusively through the process of imagining. How are you going to live with this important but troubling information about yourself and human nature?

What if you discover, as you chew on the idea that "girls should be taught that they can run great corporations," that what you wish for these girls, by way of encouragement and training, you never got yourself? What if your dream for them connects to your own deep disappointments? As valuable as the book you write on this theme may be, how much pain will the process of writing it bring you?

These are the possible outcomes associated with daring to know. You risk them, even if they frighten you, out of a pledge to know your own truth and to live courageously.

In the following exercise, you will:

1. Identify several themes or meaning threads in your life.
2. Frame an intention in support of writing about one or more of these themes.
3. Make the intention real by creating a general plan of action.
4. Move from the generality of a plan to the specifics of steps.

Making the Connection between Themes and Intention

Remember that this exercise is the ultimate in simplicity. Only your own doubts and fears will cause difficulties. Work on this exercise over the next few days.

1. Get out a pen and a piece of paper. Or sit in front of a blank computer screen. Be still, be thoughtful, and let

the themes that matter to you percolate up into consciousness. You may have to do a little work to quiet your inner demons. You may have to do a little work to achieve right silence. If questions serve as good prompts, then ask yourself questions. "What are my themes?" "What matters to me?" "Who am I in this life?"

2. Listen. Capture whatever emerges—random words, bits of phrases, visual images, odd feelings, unsettling questions.

3. Pursue your themes. Go where they take you. Clarify them. Interrogate them. Feel them. Think about them. But "do" nothing with them. Don't rush to see which of them is the best or most important. Just feel the resonances. Record your thoughts.

4. Read over what you have written. Then sleep on it. Be with your themes. Give them a chance. Let them sort themselves out.

5. Accept that your themes may disturb you. Why shouldn't they? In a way, they are about life and death. Embrace or exorcise the demons that arise to deflect you. Stay present. Accept that your themes may really be frightening.

6. When you're ready, let one theme pick you. Or consciously pick it. Neither way is inherently better. When your theme has picked you or you have picked it, say it out loud in as clear and simple a sentence as you can muster: "I will look at human nature and determine whether everyone fails when tempted." "I will see if what I want to offer girls by way of encouragement and advice amounts to a compelling piece of nonfiction."

7. Give yourself a little time, at least a minute, to see if this theme remains pressing.

8. Form a writing intention. "I am about to begin my novel about a good man." "I am about to begin a nonfiction book that encourages young girls to become great leaders."

9. Articulate a plan that goes with the intention. "I plan to begin letting this novel emerge." "I plan to spend the next year writing this book for girls, once I make sure that I really have something to say."

10. Name the steps of the plan and carry them out. Devise steps that are clear and action-filled. Where you will go? For how many hours? On which day of the week? What kind of work will you do? Name a full week's worth of tasks and carry them out.

Let's imagine how our five writers might make use of this exercise.

Amelia is embroiled in a drama with her lover and in a second drama with her employer. In the midst of all this, she isn't managing to write much. One month she does a movie review, very smart and stylish, but doesn't send it out; the next month she jots down a few pages of notes for an article about lesbian politics. Although she is maintaining a connection to her writing, she also knows that she is not honoring her unspoken pledge to write deeply.

She comes upon this exercise and decides to try it. Even though she can't find the inner peace to begin, the idea of "meaningful personal themes" starts percolating. "What are my themes?" she wonders. Then several days later, late in the afternoon at home in her apartment, she gets out her pad and formally asks herself the question: "What are the themes that concern me?" (Of course, she might ask the question differently. She might say, "Who am I?" She might say, "What really matters to me?" or "What does the world need to know that it stupidly keeps forgetting?" There is no single way to begin identifying one's themes.)

Amelia finds herself writing down a series of words and phrases: "craziness, alienation, pain, the pleasure of pain, the significance of pain, mirrors, loving women, butch, femme, rage, terror." She stops and has to keep herself from stopping completely. She isn't sure that she can pursue any of these words and phrases—they feel dangerous. But she hears herself saying, "I don't want to stop just because I'm scared." She takes a deep breath and reads over her list. Soon a pair of questions, which together feel like an insight, arises in her mind's eye. "Is it possible that I can't live without pain? Would I feel bored and inert if I didn't experience pain?"

These questions scare her but intrigue her. She begins dreaming about a novel that explores sadism and masochism. Then her thoughts shift and she begins to dream about another sort of novel, a novel about a young woman's attempt to abstain from drama. This idea flows seamlessly into another, about a girl in a mental hospital who looks forward to her shock treatments. She begins to see the ward, the room, some of the other patients. She has the sense that she's on to something. She begins to hear screams that she can't identify—she can't say whether they are screams of pain or ecstasy, or who exactly is screaming.

She discovers that she feels awake, alert, and interested. "This is cool," she says out loud. "I could write about this." She is beginning to hold a writing intention. Continuing the exercise, she makes a plan in one sentence. "I'll write about this novel for a week and see what I get." This is a good, simple plan and already further than most would-be writers get. Next Amelia spells out the steps that comprise her plan. "Today I'll jot down some notes. I'll work for an hour. Tomorrow, right after work, I'll sit my butt down in front of the computer and let the book keep happening. Friday I'll work on it at Starbucks. Saturday, a full two hours at home. Two full hours! Sunday, I'll read what I've got."

This is a fine, precise, five-step plan. If the theme proves worthy, and if Amelia can manage her inner demons, hush her mind, honor the process, and do the other things required of her, by the end of a week she may be fully embarked on a rich first novel.

Marjorie comes upon this exercise and has to smile wryly. She's attempted so many of these exercises before! But she finds the frame of this one resonant. She gets out good paper and a good pen and sits quietly. After a few minutes she finds herself growing depressed and discouraged. The problem isn't that she's bereft of ideas; the ideas that arise in her mind are plentiful and vivid. But they feel tired and stale to her. How many times has she run these exact ideas past herself? The exercise has evoked all her past writing failures and human failures, unmet dreams and unmet writing dreams. She can't stand revisiting ideas that, like the one for a certain dinosaur story and another for a historical romance set in Czarist Russia, go all the way back to her college days.

She puts away the pad and calls her mother at the nursing home to see how she's doing and if she needs anything. Then she begins her chores, in a worse mood than usual. In the back of her mind she calls herself names: hopeless, stupid, a failure. Then she recollects something written here: "A theme is more like a question than an answer." She realizes suddenly that she's always prided herself on having answers. When she took tests in school, she needed her answers to be right. She judged tests as easy or hard, not interesting or boring. Now, she wonders, isn't it finally time to stop "getting things right" and to explore her own meanings instead?

She finds this thought disconcerting but encouraging. After a few days she returns to the exercise. Again she sits with her pad open; now, instead of old ideas, nothing arrives. If this is a victory—if, that is, it signals a readiness to experience and encounter new ideas—it still only feels like blankness and emptiness. What is a "theme" or "question," she wonders, and when will one bubble up in her? Is she bereft of themes, a failure at themes? Is she, if not too stupid, then too something else, too rigid, too repressed, too . . . angry?

She hates to admit it, but she *is* angry. Very angry. More than angry—rageful. Consumed by rage. In a deep reverie, she thinks about anger. Her husband has started talking about divorce, so nasty and nonstop have her criticisms of him become. Is her criticality really a kind of misdirected anger? When she sees her husband tracking in dirt on the carpet, what about that makes her *so* angry? And her mother! She is angry enough with her mother to want to strangle her.

An image comes to her of an old woman brutally murdered. She hears the murderer's confession: "She made me angry." The murderer pauses, then continues, "Smashing my mother's face, I never felt more alive. Or better." Another pause, and then, "I'm not crazy." The detective replies, "No, but you're not so well, either." Marjorie can see the killer, who looks just like herself, but she can only hear the detective's voice. Is the detective young or middle-aged? Who is she?

She thinks that it would be very pleasant to kill off a nasty old lady in a psychological mystery. She'll have a great deal of sympathy for the murderer! But who will the detective be?

An hour later, she realizes that she's been working with some energy and enthusiasm on a mystery. Continuing the exercise, she frames her intention. "If I can come up with a detective I like, I think I'll try my hand at this mystery." She forms a general plan: "I've got a corpse and a killer—I'd better get a detective." She names her steps: "I'll spend a few hours at the mystery bookstore, checking on popular sleuths. No doubt mine needs an unusual occupation, an intriguing setting, something. So, I'll look at a few successful mysteries and see what girl detectives do for a living. That'll be tomorrow. Meantime, I'll make a list of my own passions and areas of expertise, to see if one of them works for . . . sleuth Sandy. Maybe I'll do that right now. I think I should also write down what I know about the book already. Then, I guess I should set up a writing schedule. And . . . I don't think I'll call Mother today!"

Sam, no closer to a dissertation idea today than yesterday, resists trying this exercise. He would still rather wait for inspiration and a dissertation idea to strike him than to wrestle one into existence. Nor, as he reads over the exercise before discarding it, has he a clue what his themes or meaning threads are or even what's meant by "theme" or "meaning thread." Besides, why would he need to understand or uncover them just to do a business-oriented dissertation? This is business, after all, not literature or philosophy!

Nonetheless, with his deadline approaching, one hot summer day Sam surrenders. He submits to the process and starts to wonder about life, about the big questions, about his past and his thoughts and feelings. This is strange and new, and he finds it surprisingly pleasant and unthreatening. He begins to think about his dad's alcoholism, about the fights and scenes around his parents' kitchen table, about learning at the last minute, from his stepmom and not his dad, about his dad's decision not to help him with college tuition.

Then a business-related idea pops into his head. Do workers work better if they're emotionally supported?

He recognizes instantly that his question is really enormously complicated. If you come from a harsh environment, if you grow up believing that it's a dog-eat-dog world out there, then maybe a harsh business environment would suit you best. What feels like emotional support to one person might feel like intrusiveness to another. What about gender differences? And cultural differences? Mightn't a raise and a nice bonus compensate for a lot of emotional pain?

Suddenly Sam sees that he's been hoping to arrive at an answer—a good dissertation idea—without asking any good questions. He has to laugh a little, for this is the identical pit his boss fell into when he chose the company's new computer system. His boss went for the best system, one using the latest German software and an aggressively marketed server, without ever asking the simplest questions, like "Will this system really meet our needs?"

Sam sets down some of these basic questions with respect to

his burgeoning idea. "What are a worker's needs?" "Does it pay to honor those needs?" "What's an 'emotional need' anyway?" "Might companies become more profitable if they met workers' emotional needs right off the bat and made them the highest priority, even higher than salary and benefits? If so, wouldn't such a program actually save companies money?" "Mightn't it work to provide employees with more happiness and fewer bonuses?"

Sam recognizes that these are interesting questions, objectively interesting and also interesting to him. He forms an intention: to better understand what "the emotional support of employees" might mean. He states his general plan: "I'll spend the next few weeks investigating this idea, keeping good track of it and making sure that it still feels as smart as it feels right now. And I won't choose a hypothesis too soon—I'll keep an open mind about that. Maybe emotional support is a good thing, and maybe it isn't a good thing, and maybe it all depends on how I define it. We'll see."

Sam articulates the steps of his plan. He'll commit four hours Monday evening to searching the Internet, to see what he can find on the subject of the emotional support of employees. Tuesday he'll spend a few hours looking for the same information in the business section of his local bookstore. Wednesday he'll see what he's learned and begin to write out tentative answers to the question, "How should 'emotional support in a business environment' be conceived?" He knows that his final dissertation topic, shaped by the desires of his committee, may end up having little do with the emotional needs of employees. But at the very least he'll have worked on something personally meaningful for a week, and that work may also lead him to just the right topic.

Anne, existential and ethical by nature, is very close to her own themes. Ideas come to her all the time, and some have served her well as the grains of sand around which pearls of writing have coalesced. But at this point in her writing career she wants more than a good idea. She knows the motivating power and intrinsic worth of a good theme, but she's been there and done that. Now she wants an idea to build a best-seller around.

But that's much easier said than done. Because, as a deep writer, she can't embark on a project that has no depth and worth beyond its marketability, even a "bestseller idea" must still meet her strict standards. She's faced this dilemma before and, staring the requirements of bestseller fiction straight in the eye, she's always blinked. She's turned away from formula and the demands of the escapist popular reader toward her own themes and meanings.

She's not sure how this exercise might serve her, but she finds the idea of life themes interesting enough to pursue. Several pop up, and she jots them down: the mysterious passage of information between women (she might write a book in which the women are mute but still communicate perfectly), the tenuousness of friendship and its all-too-frequent demise (the book might be about a good friendship that ends in a bad betrayal), the lack of viability of the modern couple (here she might posit the ideal couple, a wise, well-matched pair, and show how even their marriage can fracture and collapse), and animal instincts colliding with the postmodern culture (the book she envisions is one involving a woman lost in the wilds whose instincts desert her, a kind of upside-down *Naked Prey* for women).

This quick list surprises her. She actually likes all her ideas! All of them interest her. All feel worthy. But how many people would buy books based on these themes? To judge by her past sales figures, maybe ten or fifteen thousand. And ten or fifteen thousand are a hundred thousand too few. Still, she loves the ideas she's just generated. An intention arises: to pursue a theme of real richness and meaning, maybe even one of those she's just come up with, to write deeply, honorably, and honestly, but also to frame and fashion her work in a way compelling to a mass audience. Can she do this? That's the eternal question!

She finds her first step appalling but necessary: to spend an afternoon in a chain bookstore strategically browsing bestselling women's fiction. She knows just which inner demons this visit will activate—feelings of envy, a vision of herself as a failure, a sense that others can effortlessly play a game whose rules she either doesn't understand or refuses to understand. But rather than erase this step from her list, she underlines it.

No other steps come to her. But then a writing assignment pops into her head. "I think I should describe women as seen by other women. Fictional characters describing other fictional characters. Nancy describing Joan. Joan describing Mary. Mary describing Ellen. Etc." She isn't perfectly sure what this assignment is about, but she's written enough to trust that something is brewing just out of conscious awareness. She can even articulate a little what's on her mind. "To write bestselling fiction, I'll probably need a repertory company of women and not just the women I'm drawn to writing about. I'll probably also have to write about them in some unfamiliar way, through the eyes of a romance novelist, a magical realist writer, or some other such person. So, this exercise."

These two steps—to visit a bookstore and browse, and to sketch some unfamiliar women—flesh out her plan. They feel like a lot and enough. Acting on her plan, she packs up for an afternoon of bookstore legwork and note-taking.

Henry is in crisis. He finds it startling, upsetting, and frightening that, well into his fifties, sex is more on his mind than ever. Nor is it simply sex. It is the dark underbelly of sex that's consuming him: cruel sex, ironic sex, humiliating sex, irrational sex. In the midst of a hectic, even insane bicoastal life, with apartments and lovers East and West, with too much alcohol, too many drugs, and, above all, too many obsessions tormenting him, he dreams of somehow recovering a measure of the integrity he feels he once had. What he hates most about himself is the way he's taken to glamorizing cruelty in his screenplays and stage plays. This tendency he finds downright despicable. He knows he's got to do something, and he thinks that probably it should be something spiritual, maybe a sweat lodge ceremony or a vision quest. But he tries this exercise instead.

As unused to this sort of creative wrestling as he is, Henry stays with it. While no themes come to him, a realization does. He begins to sense that he's taken the easy way out in virtually all of his recent writing and that his motivation throughout his career has been a need for critical acclaim and success. He's never seen it so clearly before, but now he does: he's always wanted to be popular.

It dawns on him that he would like to be honest for a

change. But how can a man change his stripes just like that? Can he locate his own truth under the facade he's built up over a lifetime, while his obsessions and compulsions wreak their havoc? Just thinking about it makes him crave drugs and sex. He stops the exercise abruptly, not sure if he's depressed, disgusted, or aroused. He does know that he wants some Scotch.

As he gets up to pour himself a drink and quiet his nerves, it suddenly comes to him that he would like to write a nonfiction book, maybe an interview book with photographs, in which he poses but refuses to give an easy answer to the question, "What is bisexuality?" The very unanswerability of the question takes his breath away. But irony and cynicism quickly submerge the awe. "Who am I to write such a book? I only want sex, not knowledge!" And, "Which closeted Hollywood bisexual can I get to play the lead?" And, "With songs, it'll play on Broadway for years!" But inside him a battle rages between cynicism and hope.

A title comes to him: *Men Who Sleep with Women . . . And with Men.* Instantly he wonders if it shouldn't be *Men Who Sleep with Men . . . And with Women.* As if that isn't exactly the issue! As if a horn of the dilemma isn't the possibility that he'll never know which title to choose! But this line of thought pleases him. He has the feeling that this inner dialogue, laced with irony as it is, still has a human face to it.

He frames his intention: "I will write uncynically about bisexuality, not to glamorize it and not to defend it, but just to . . ." Many times he tries to finish the sentence, but he discovers that he can't. Finally he surrenders. "I don't know the answer. I'll have to find out." This conclusion feels strange, provocative, and alarming. Before, when he wrote, he knew all the plot twists, how to describe the screenplay in a smart sentence, where the commercials went in the teleplay, when to insert a laugh. Not knowing feels weird . . . but richer and better than knowing.

He frames his plan: "I will write a truthful nonfiction book about bisexuality. What it's otherwise about, I have no idea."

His first step, he decides, is to paste up a pair of pictures, one of an attractive woman and the second of an attractive man, on the wall beside his computer. His idea is to be with these pictures, to see how they affect him, and maybe to learn something from his reaction to them. His second step is to start to read the popular literature on bisexuality. He has the sense that most of it will be too partisan, too simple, or just wrongheaded and false, but he reckons he'll have to familiarize himself with it sooner or later.

It takes him a while to dream up some additional steps, but then they come to him all at once: to spend a few hours each day writing from the heart instead of from the head; to consciously empty himself of the writing tricks he's learned over the years; and to write without irony. He recognizes that these steps lack precision, but they seem, at least, to be coming from a place of uncharacteristic genuineness. If this chapter were a fairy tale, Henry would skip the whiskey. He doesn't. But he only has a single large one, instead of several, which is itself a first victory.

One Writer's Intention

Here's how an actual writer struggled to remain motivated and carry out her intention in the face of longstanding self-doubt. She wrote me the following letter:

I teach literature and creative writing to eleventh- and twelfth-graders. Each year I beg to get the "low" classes. These are kids who hate school, don't want to be there, and usually hate their English classes the most. They feel stupid, and they are all shoved into this same class, with their low performance skills being the one thing they all have in common.

To me, they are all diamonds in the rough!! Still!! After twenty-eight years. I love these kids. Working with them makes me feel truly alive. The challenge is a creative one, and I love it. What is the key that will work with this one . . . and that one . . . What about that one?! Very exciting.

Can I make voracious readers out of them? They come into my class having read one or no books ever. The first thing they find out is that they will be reading a novel for the first twenty minutes in class EVERY day until June! This freaks them out!

But 95 percent of them get totally hooked because of JUST ONE WRITER. That writer is R. L. Stine. He's written maybe fifty or sixty teenage murder mysteries that are SO mesmerizing FROM THE VERY FIRST SENTENCE that these kids (most of them suffering from dyslexia or attention deficit disorder or problems that have no name yet) get hooked and go into shock when they actually complete the first book in a couple of weeks. They proudly come up at the start of each weekend to check out the book for the weekend because they simply MUST find out what happens next!!!

So one summer, I read twelve of Stine's books one right after the other, and I began to see the elements that made his books so exciting to teenagers. I decided to try writing my own murder mystery, using some of the elements Stine utilized, including short, direct sentences and a nonstop plot.

My problem is (and this is going to sound so stupid, probably) that I'm very affected by others' responses to the project. I play golf with a woman who teaches English at a college, and when I told her I was currently working on a little murder mystery for teenagers, one along the lines of what Stine writes, she said, "You've got to be kidding! Why don't you write a good book?" Another friend who writes and paints responded with, "But you're really a good writer. Why would you want to drop down to that level when you could write so much better?" My dad's concern is always money. He wanted to know how much money I could make on a little teenage novel compared to the amount I could make writing a successful adult novel.

Using an exercise from my book *Fearless Creating,* she crafted the following vision statement, which she put up where she could see it on the wall beside her computer.

There is a large segment of our teenage population that could fall through the cracks as adults, because they are unable to read and write at the level it takes to successfully survive in today's world. These warm, playful, beautiful kids are classified as illiterate.

They need "bridges."

Bridges are gifted people and methods that make it possible for these eager, joyful children to leap from a narrow, limited world to one that is rich in possibility.

A few skilled teachers perform this miracle every year. And they enlist the help of enlightened writers of teenage fiction to accomplish this miracle. What some people perceive as nothing more than "escape fiction" is, in reality, a golden bridge to the magic land of possibility. Reluctant readers become voracious readers.

Because of these powerful teachers and writers, our world becomes enriched by the beautiful gifts that these teenagers then bestow on us as they enter adulthood.

My own personal mission in this world, in this incarnation, is to join hands with these teachers and writers . . . these bridges . . . and add my own light, love, and energy to the mysterious unfolding drama that we call Life.

With her vision statement posted in front of her as a reminder of her themes and intention, she began on her "little" murder mystery—which, as I write this, she's almost completed.

Making
Choices

A writer has a million choices to make: whether to choose this idiosyncratic idea or that one, whether to paint her hero's study Chinese red or cobalt blue, whether to tackle racism in her novel or the sadomasochistic love affair she experienced last winter. Every word is a choice, every plot twist is a choice, every character trait is a choice.

All these myriad choices notwithstanding, the primary choice a writer makes is the following: whether to write for herself or for the marketplace. Will she or won't she strive to be a popular writer as well as a deep writer? This is a crucial choice, more important than all her other choices put together.

Let's say that you manage to write and sell a book every single year, which would be a terrific accomplishment. Each of those books is likely to earn you no more than five, ten, or fifteen thousand dollars in royalties. Can you live on that? Surely not. You could have what looks like an extremely successful writing career, with dozens and even scores of books published, all the while needing to work a day job or fashion a second career in order to make ends meet. Or let's imagine that you received advances even better than average, say more in the twenty-, twenty-five-, or thirty-thousand-dollar range. Could you live on that? Maybe barely. But what if it took you two years to write one of your books, not one? You'd be back in the ten- or fifteen-thousand-dollar-a-year range, back below the poverty level. I think you see what I'm getting at. Only the most popular authors earn a living by writing.

The advances for my last eight books have been, in the order I received them: eighteen, fifteen, twenty, twenty, seven, twenty-five, three, twenty, and eight thousand dollars. Some of these books have earned additional royalties, and some haven't yet. These modest numbers do not generate much excitement among agents, editors, or writers with stars in their eyes, but they are real numbers earned by a working writer. They are real advances for real books in the real world.

Can a person live on these amounts? Certainly not. The other day I read in the newspaper that a "middle-class" income in the San Francisco Bay Area, where I live, is defined as between sixty and one hundred thousand dollars annually. Virtually no writer, even those with a name you might recognize, is earning that kind of money. Even writers who sell a hundred thousand copies of a book do that only once or twice in a lifetime. The rule is not ironclad, but it is very simple: a writer can't live by writing. And imagine if one were a poet!

The deep writer is not a materialist. But he also doesn't want to live in poverty. As important as writing with integrity is, writers aren't better equipped than anyone else to survive in a cardboard box under the freeway. So they do what they can to make some money. Sometimes they teach, often part-time. But that doesn't make much of a difference. I teach one class a semester at a well-respected college and earn three thousand dollars a semester, or six thousand dollars a year. Others try repairing bicycles or leading retreats or workshops. Some do mainstream things that pay a living wage, becoming directors of environmental nonprofits or corporate attorneys. But they find that those fourteen-hour days prevent them from writing. Every writer is forced to try his hand at this or that, looking for answers, and many writers spend a lifetime looking for a reasonable solution that allows for both a writing life and a heated apartment without ever quite finding one.

My solution is that I am married to a woman who earns a living wage. Before that I was helped by the GI Bill and by my mother. In every writer's life are facts and sentences like these. When writers, and those who would counsel writers, ignore these realities, they get into trouble. If a writer has a legacy, an independent income, or a working spouse, or if, on the other hand, a writer must write training manuals or work in a bank to pay the bills, these are very important facts. To ignore them is to act as if one could live on air and dreams alone.

The financial side of the matter is one important thing. The emotional side is another. How good does it feel to write and not get published? Say that you spend your time from age twenty to twenty-four writing an eccentric, personal first novel, which you put into the marketplace at a time cold to first novels, such that all agents and editors who do not send you form rejections say that, through no fault of yours or theirs, your novel can't be published. This news prompts you to start on a second novel, which you plan to write a little more strategically but which still turns out personal and idiosyncratic, so that you now have two novels that can't be sold. Now you're nearing thirty and faced with the question: "What in God's name am I supposed to do next?" The answer you find in your heart is much more likely to be "Jump off a bridge!" than "Start on a third novel!"

These two conundrums, the practical and the emotional, dog writers all their lives. A third conundrum, having to do with ethics and intellectual integrity, dogs the deep writer as well. Not only does it not feel good to write a book filled with quarter-truths and outright lies, it doesn't feel too ethical either. Yes, it's exciting to contemplate selling a gullible public two million copies of your chats with angels or aliens, but, I mean, *really!* Yes, it would be wonderful to make some thoroughly outrageous claim in your title— *Heal Yourself Instantly! Live Forever! Become a Genius!*—and then promote your book like a fiend and become a media star and a reigning expert. But the deep writer has trouble aiming for successes of this sort.

Happily, the principles of competition do not so favor the popular writer that the deep writer, possessing a brain and a will, can't at least think about competing. Maybe she can't write one kind of popular book, but what about another kind, one that looks and smells like it belongs on a bestseller list by virtue of its title and its willingness to open its arms to readers? The deep writer may not be able to compete on even terms with the popular writer, who has the larger audience ready and waiting, but she can at least make the conscious decision to think about competing.

Thinking about Choices

This chapter is about choosing. Writers must and will make choices: to write or not to write, to tackle a book or an article, to write for professionals or a lay audience, to write in the first person or the third person.

The primary choice under discussion here is the choice a writer makes to write deeply and also popularly; that is, the choice a writer makes to write with one eye on the marketplace. Is such a choice possible for the deep writer? Will her psyche allow for it? Will agents and editors see through her half-hearted attempts at formula work or genre writing and cry, "Gotcha!" Is there a way for a deep writer both to aim for success and to write deeply?

I am not saying the answer is yes, and I am not saying the answer is no. I think there is an outside chance, no more but also no less, that you can write deeply and also find commercial success.

Sometimes successful writers give young writers the following advice: they smile and say, "Follow your bliss; write what's in your heart; don't listen to anyone about anything or worry about the marketplace; just be true to yourself." I'm not implying that the experienced writer is lying to you because she thinks of you as a rival and wants you to fail. But I don't think she's telling you the unvarnished truth.

It's true that the successful writer who gives such advice may have been just unaccountably lucky, rather than devious, crafty, or self-promoting. But it would be nice if he or she would confess that. "I was just lucky. I had this friend who knew this agent, and this agent knew this editor who right at that second was looking for a novel about lesbian werewolves who emigrate to Jupiter, so I got a huge advance for my first novel, which caused a great stir in the media and helped sell the book later on. Plus by coincidence the publicist was a lesbian werewolf herself who dropped everything to promote my book like mad, coupled with the fact that, for whatever reason, I struck a deep chord with women readers who, it turns out, have an affinity for lesbian werewolves, and so, yes, do write whatever you like, but also get very, very lucky. Have the right friend who herself has the right friend, and make sure that what you're writing resonates in a primitive way with book-buying women."

It's possible that this writer never did think about her potential audience, either in or out of conscious awareness, as she was writing her book. Conceivably, she really was writing entirely for herself and then got lucky. But imagine another writer who makes this same claim with less justification. This writer has been making marketplace choices all along, aiming her work at buyers but walling that information off from herself. She's then able to say with a straight face, "I just write what I like, and people seem to respond to it." Some of our more successful nonfiction writers today, who are likely to have backgrounds in marketing or public relations and not in the field in which they write, are probably engaged in this kind of self-deception. If you asked them, "Are you making outrageous claims just to sell books?" they would say "No!" and probably pass a lie detector test.

I know a successful ceramic sculptor whose art is very popular. She claims not to be interested in the marketplace. She says she just does what her heart tells her to do. But if you ask her, for example, why her cats curl up in their trademark way—I'm making this up, she doesn't sculpt cats—she will tell you, buyers like curled cats, not uncurled cats. Curled cats fetch X dollars, and uncurled cats, if you could sell one, would only fetch Y dollars. Despite her disclaimers, it turns out that she both understands the marketplace and makes things wanted in the marketplace. That she is doing work she claims to love that coincidentally sells is not, I think, a happy accident, but an unconscious choice that she keeps unconscious so that she can avoid the charge that she is crassly compromising.

I tend to talk to writers about these matters directly. I say, "You may not be writing your current novel because your heart is hurt over the fact that your first two novels never got published. Do you want to try your hand at popular fiction now? Do you want to aim straight at the marketplace?" Writers never take this as a veiled accusation or an insult. They may still want to write in their own way, trying a third and a fourth time to do exactly what interests them, but they also know that their depressed finances and their other depressions are inextricably linked to choices of this sort.

I saw a new client this morning. A therapist who grew up in South America and came to the United States as an adult, this woman reported a personal history of childhood abuse, multiple personality disorder, and eating disorders. She wanted to write about these three issues and their effects on her life. She also wanted to explain how she helps clients with these issues. On top of that, she wanted to include her thoughts about her own therapy, her spiritual renewal, and her struggles with her sexuality. She hoped to connect all these matters in memoir form. She had an introduction and three chapters already written, which she'd sent to me in anticipation of our meeting. I found them compelling and well written.

As we discussed her options, I said the following. "You could certainly write this book as a memoir, but, even though a few memoirs did very well last season, they are still hard to sell. You could write a popular self-help book about multiple personality disorder, ritual child abuse, or eating disorders, but I checked with a literary agent this morning and she confirmed what I suspected, that none of these topics is much wanted at the moment. My hunch is that your best bet of writing a commercially salable book is to focus on something you just said to me, that eating disorders and a history of childhood abuse often go hand in hand, and to direct the book to the large audience of men and women who are overweight. You could make the controversial statement that overeating and childhood abuse are very often related, and take to the talk shows with the thesis that dieting may not work unless childhood trauma issues are addressed. In effect, you would be writing a diet book—maybe in collaboration with a nutritionist—and new diet books are always wanted."

Maybe she will write a personal memoir, or maybe she will write a book designed for the marketplace. I have no investment in either outcome: let me be clear about that. Deep writing is what I wanted from her and what I want from you. But if you can find the way to do both, to write deeply and also to frame your book strategically, you will have made a choice with pleasant marketplace consequences.

Framing Your Book

Hold your arms out in front of you and bend them comfortably at the elbows, turning your palms upward. What you are doing is making a kind of scale out of your being, using your palms to hold quantities you'll be weighing in each hand. Practice by raising and lowering each palm, sensing how they feel when they're out of balance with each other and when they're in balance.

Now imagine that in one palm you're holding the word "deep" and in the other palm the word "strategic." Substitute whatever words resonate for you: "personal," "thoughtful," or "idiosyncratic"; "popular," "bestselling," or "commercial." Bring these two quantities, these two ideas, into balance. Feel the weight of each; feel especially how they want to come into balance, how that feels like the most comfortable position of all. Whenever you write a piece that you hope will be both deep and popular, bring out your personal scale. Feel any imbalance, and ask yourself the question, "What do I need to do to strike a better balance?"

Let's say that you want to write strategically or that you at least want to think about that possibility. Let's also say, for the sake of this discussion, that you have a nonfiction self-help book in mind, because in that genre we see most clearly how a popular book can be manufactured. Probably, to start with, you would only have a broad subject or a vague idea in mind. It might be "something about incest" or "something about sibling rivalry." It might have to do with spirituality, aging, or parent-child relationships. Maybe you've taught for many years and feel ready to describe some successful teaching techniques.

Maybe there's something important you've learned from your divorce that you feel is worth communicating to others.

Many would-be self-help writers get to this point and no further. They have a dream of writing and a vague idea about what they want to write about, but they can't proceed. The following exercise can help such writers move forward, because it reveals how every subject is really a multitude of subjects, slightly different or very different from one another depending on the "frame" or point of view chosen. It also shows how the marketplace can be taken into consideration naturally and even effortlessly.

Take a look at the following twenty-five frames. What they represent will become clearer to you when you see the examples that follow. For now, just read them over.

1. Newness
2. Simplification
3. Ease
4. Comprehensiveness
5. Demystification
6. Increases
7. Connecting a philosophy or religion with a subject
8. Personal creativity
9. Mood management
10. Lifespan vitality
11. Psychological health and healing
12. Specific psychological disorders
13. Mind/body integration
14. Spirituality
15. Personal effectiveness

16. Time management
17. Relationship management
18. Community building
19. Value building
20. Confidence building
21. Rootedness
22. Process
23. Strategies
24. Categories
25. Alternative approaches

Mary, a career counselor at a small college in a Midwestern town, has had the desire to write for the longest time, ever since childhood. But she's fallen into the trap I described: the subject she'd like to write about, somehow related to her career counseling experiences, feels too big and too amorphous to tackle. She knows that she's helped hundreds of people find jobs and that she must have a lot to say about her way of working, and she also knows that whenever she picks up a book in her field she has the same reaction: I could write that! But she hasn't started writing yet.

Mary comes upon the following exercise: create twenty-five titles that sound like titles you'd see in your local bookstore, connecting your subject up with each of the twenty-five frames just listed. These are the book titles Mary creates.

1. Newness
   Job Hunting the Modern Way
2. Simplification
   Everybody's Basic Guide to Job Hunting

3. Ease
   Job Hunting Made Easy
4. Comprehensiveness
   Mary Smith's Complete Guide to Job Hunting
5. Demystification
   Job Hunting Secrets Your Counselor Never Told You
6. Increases
   Double Your Job Prospects!
7. Connecting a philosophy or religion with a subject
   The Tao of Job Hunting
8. Personal creativity
   Job Hunting on the Right Side of the Brain
9. Mood management
   Conquering the Job-Hunting Blues
10. Lifespan vitality
    Exciting Work After Fifty!
11. Psychological health and healing
    Find a Job Without Losing Your Mind
12. Specific psychological disorders
    Ending Interview Phobia
13. Mind/body integration
    The Holistic Job Search
14. Spirituality
    Job Hunting with Soul
15. Personal Effectiveness
    The Eight Skills of Effective Job Hunters
16. Time management
    Your Perfect Resume in Twenty Minutes Flat!
17. Relationship management
    People Hire People

18. Community building
    Networking with Heart
19. Value building
    The Ten Commandments of Job Hunting
20. Confidence building
    Affirmations for Job Hunters
21. Rootedness
    Work Where You Live
22. Process
    Seven Steps to Successful Job Hunting
23. Strategies
    Solution-Focused Job Hunting
24. Categories
    Employers Are from Earth, Job Hunters Are from Pluto
25. Alternative approaches
    Great Jobs Through the Back Door

She looks at her list and can't believe her eyes. For the first time she sees how a big subject can become a manageable subject by virtue of some simple focusing. Not only could she write just about any of these books, two or three of them actually interest her. She herself uses affirmations, and she could surely write a book called *Affirmations for Job Hunters*. As a student of Taoist poetry and philosophy, she finds *The Tao of Job Hunting* another natural. This way of framing a book never occurred to her, but now that she's tried her hand at it, it feels as if a veil has been lifted from her eyes. She still has choices to make: which of these books she really wants to write, which would have the best chance in the marketplace, whether her first choice has been done to death already, and many more.

But these are choices with an inviting, rather than a terrifying, feel to them.

Consider Mark. Mark is trying to switch careers. He's sold things his whole life, all the while hoping for a better, more fulfilling career. Recently he's begun consulting with some of his friends who also sell, doing informal workshops on the subject of building confidence. He feels some conflict about this, because he's not really sure that he wants to spend his time helping people do a better job of selling, but by the same token he finds it too arrogant to dismiss all the decent salespeople he knows out of hand. So, although he isn't all that confident himself and although some residue of a conflict remains, he leads more of these workshops. After a while he begins to think about writing a book on the subject.

He comes upon this exercise and gives it a try, saying to himself, "I'll get 'confidence' into every title and be bold in my claims!" He generates the following list:

1. Newness
   Brand New Confidence for Today's Salesperson!
2. Simplification
   Sales Confidence Made Simple
3. Ease
   Grow Confident While You Cat Nap Between Customers!
4. Comprehensiveness
   Total Confidence for Salespeople
5. Demystification
   Secrets of the Confident Salesperson
6. Increases
   Triple Your Sales Confidence!

7. Connecting a philosophy or religion with a subject
   Zen Confidence in the Showroom
8. Personal creativity
   Creating Confident Salespeople
9. Mood management
   Beat the Prospecting Blues with Confidence
10. Lifespan vitality
    Confident Selling After Fifty
11. Psychological health and healing
    Cure Sales Burnout with Confidence!
12. Specific psychological disorders
    Overcome Your Cold Calling Phobia with Confidence
13. Mind/body integration
    Holistic Selling with Confidence
14. Spirituality
    The Soul of Sales Confidence
15. Personal effectiveness
    Sell the Confident Way
16. Time management
    One Hour to Greater Sales Confidence!
17. Relationship management
    Increasing Customer Confidence
18. Community building
    Building Confidence and Community in Your Sales Force
19. Value building
    Confidence Is a Sales Virtue!
20. Confidence building
    Five Steps to Selling with Confidence
21. Rootedness
    Confident Selling to Friends and Neighbors

22. Process
     The Eight Stages of Confidence Building for Salespeople
23. Strategies
     Affirming the Confident Sales Life
24. Categories
     Confident Seller, Happy Buyer
25. Alternative approaches
     Thirty Unusual Ways to Gain Confidence in the Sales Arena

Like Mary, Mark sees how each title represents a different frame, a different choice, and different possibilities and liabilities. He has already begun to create steps, stages, and tactics in his workshops, and *Five Steps to Selling with Confidence, The Eight Stages of Confidence Building for Salespeople,* and *Thirty Unusual Ways to Gain Confidence in the Sales Arena* all sound attractive to him. Of course, he has no idea what the real number of steps, stages, or ways are: he's just made them up for the sake of this exercise. Maybe he's got twelve strategies to offer, or maybe he's got thirty. Maybe there are six stages and not eight stages, or eleven steps and not five. All that can be worked out. His own confidence grows as he contemplates the essential ease with which a book of this sort might be constructed.

He suddenly realizes what titles of this sort seem to promise and what they actually do promise. At their most grandiose and hyperbolic, they seem to offer the sun and the moon. Yet book buyers understand that a book can't be called *Maybe You Can Become a Tiny Bit More Confident if You Try Really Hard* or *An Investigation of the Effects of Cognitive Techniques on Confidence-Building in the Statistically Average Person.* It has to be called something like *Total Confidence!* The deep writer, who hates the idea of hyperbolic titles and baseless promises, doesn't have to worry that book buyers are taking such a title literally. All readers are hoping for is a book that will be reasonably useful.

Total Confidence, when done by a deep writer, would only have to do a serious job of communicating how readers could become somewhat more confident. The deep writer would do an honorable, common-sense job, offering sound advice and effective strategies. Between its covers, it would stop its sales pitch and just do good work. Readers, who might gain something from such a book, would have very little chance of encountering it unless the writer had framed her subject in such a way that interested agents, editors, and the book-buying public.

Questions of "truth in advertising" are of real concern to the deep writer, who is first and foremost an ethicist. They are not to be taken lightly or dismissed with a shrug. As I was finishing writing my book *Staying Sane in the Arts,* when a final decision about its title had to be made, I was asked if I felt comfortable calling it *Staying Sane and Solvent in the Arts.* My publisher's marketing director wanted a title that offered a promise of that sort. But I had to say no. I felt that I was offering a way for creative and performing artists to make sense of the psychological challenges they face, but I couldn't begin to promise them a path to solvency. That felt like a line I couldn't cross.

It's easy to see how an exercise of this sort works for a subject like job hunting or confident selling. But what if a writer's subject is more nebulous or ambiguous? What if he is ambivalent about the promises he can honorably make? What if he has virtually no promises to make, only difficult, even unanswerable questions to pose? Even then, this framing exercise has its value. Its playfulness is a good antidote to the heaviness and heavy-heartedness that so often accompany contemplation of our complex, often contradictory ideas.

Consider the predicament of John, the executive director of a nonprofit environmental organization. He possesses a love of nature and a real concern for environmental issues, but his philosophical attitude distinguishes him from many other activists. He feels confused about how to balance the rights of squirrels with the rights of lumberjacks: are squirrels really as important as people? For that matter, are people really as important as squirrels? He's confused as to whether we are all sacred creatures or throwaways, and whether human consciousness endows us with special privileges or responsibilities; and he has a million other questions that either can't be answered neatly or can't be answered to his satisfaction.

He senses that he has a book to write about all of this, but how can he write a book when he hardly knows what he feels? He tries this framing exercise anyway, not to arrive at a best-selling title but just to loosen himself up, to have a little absurd fun, to begin to play with the thoughts that have been percolating inside of him for years. In this spirit—part playful, part ironic, part skeptical, part hopeful—he generates the following list. As he thinks about each title, he actually gains clarity about his personal philosophies.

1. Newness
   Environmental Activism for Today
   "Boring," he thinks. "Yawn. And it isn't what I have in mind."

2. Simplification
   Environmental Activism for Idiots
   "Not bad. You could sell some good, simple ideas in such a book, the usual composting, recycling, act locally, think globally things. I don't find this offensive."
3. Ease
   Save the Earth Without Leaving Your Couch!
   "Hm. I'm impressed. I should probably throw in world peace."
4. Comprehensiveness
   How to Save Every Leaf, Bug, and Pond!
   "What a mouthful! I think not."
5. Demystification
   Ten Secrets of an Environmental Activist
   "What's this one about? Maybe a how-to guide for fledgling nonprofits? Or guerrilla tactics for environmental activists? Could be some possibilities here . . ."
6. Increases
   Increase the Ozone Layer by 100 Percent!
   "I like that! I could bash car emission standards, factory emission standards, the industrial revolution itself. But it still doesn't speak to what's in my heart."
7. Connecting a philosophy or religion with a subject
   Your Sun Signs and the Environment
   "Capricorn, this is your day to think about rain forests . . ."
8. Personal creativity
   Creative Ecology
   "Let's see, a few painting exercises, a little journaling about your fears and hopes for the environment—"

9. Mood management
   Environmental Blues
   "Hm. This one feels interesting. I do believe that environmental consciousness and depression go hand in hand. What if I suggest that, rather than looking at 'environmental depression' as a tragedy, we consider it useful information that helps us understand why it's hard for the average person to get involved and why activists burn out? I bet I could suggest some answers—maybe even learn some answers for myself!"

On John goes. He discovers that he may have something important to say and that he may be able to find a way to say it. He has the experiences and credentials to write an important book, and maybe now he can find the right framework. He sees that he doesn't have to write a book called *Save a Whale in Six Minutes Flat,* but that even if he should stoop to such a title he might still be able to tell his honest story within that book's pages. As he thinks about this, a working title for his book suddenly comes to him: *From Here to Ecology.* It makes him smile. He doesn't know what the book will be about, but he has the sense that it will be about something.

Serving Two Masters

It may seem as if we've veered off in a strange direction, toward bestsellerdom and marketplace mania, when we started off on achieving a quiet mind and holding a deep writing intention. But remember that you have two objectives in mind and two masters to serve: to write deeply, but to write something that has a chance in the marketplace. It doesn't matter if that marketplace is the marketplace of literary magazines, academic journals, regional presses, or large New York City publishers. To have readers is to serve a second master in addition to yourself.

Writers in the real world tend to make one of the following choices:

1. "I do not care about success in the marketplace or access to the marketplace. I am writing my work the way it needs to be written."
2. "I care about success in the marketplace and access to the marketplace, but still I mean to write my work the way it needs to be written. Perhaps a miracle will occur and my poem, story, article, or book will be wanted despite its disregard for commercial expectations."
3. "I care about success in the marketplace, and I will strive to make my writing commercially viable. This may mean that my ideas may cease to exist in their original form and that only a portion of their depth will be retained. But I can live with that."

Do you find one of these positions more satisfactory than the others? Are there better variations? Can you retain your intellectual honesty and morals while meeting the demands of the marketplace? Should you try to write "somewhere in the middle," bending this way for the sake of your reading public and bending the other way for the sake of truthfulness—all this bending and swaying resulting, one fears, in work that is neither fish nor fowl? I suppose when all is said and done I am saying the following: deep writing is one thing and career considerations are another, but it is hard not to want to think about both and find some way to craft a happy marriage between them.

If you don't think this is a puzzle harder to solve than the most diabolical mathematical brain twister, you haven't tried living the writing life. Early one recent morning, driving home from dropping off my oldest daughter at school, I saw a taxi pull up to the curb on a deserted suburban street. The first sentence of a new novel came to me. "Taxis in suburbia always augur strange events: a mad aunt's unannounced visit, the return of the prodigal, or something equally sinister." I felt I could launch right into this novel, learning what it was about as I began to write it. But these days I choose not to write such novels. They are too hard to sell. Am I saying that you shouldn't write them? No. Am I saying that you should write them? No. Am I straddling the fence? Yes!

Yesterday I received an angry letter from a painter in Italy about my book *Affirmations for Artists*. Toward the middle of the letter he wrote:

Especially on the question of painting for the market and painting for yourself, you're squarely on the fence. What's wrong with painting junk that sells if it satisfies the painter? And isn't an artistic heritage richer because of some artists who refused to cater to an audience? I once took a psychology class and quickly learned that I could get top grades simply by identifying the weasel-worded answer among the multiple choices. Your affirmations reminded me of those weasel-worded answers. Is this a characteristic of therapists?

I *am* straddling the fence, advocating neither the purely personal nor the purely commercial, because both choices leave a lot to be desired. With the first, the likelihood is great that what you write will not be wanted or will be wanted in a limited way, and psychological pain accompanies this outcome. With the second, you may well feel that you've violated some important ethical principles and are likely to experience psychological discomfort as a result. The most satisfactory path, extremely difficult to negotiate but not impossible, is to strive to marry the deep and the commercial in such a way that your truth gets told and also reaches a wide audience.

Our Writers Begin to Choose

At the point where we left them, our five writers had each formed a writing intention, mapped out a beginning plan, and begun to think about their projects. Amelia was thinking about a novel set in an insane asylum. Marjorie started on a mystery at whose heart was her own anger with her mother. Sam set out to do research on the subject of the emotional support of employees. Anne decided to do character sketches of unfamiliar women and to check out the requirements of bestseller fiction. Henry toyed with the idea of investigating his own bisexuality.

Had they factored the marketplace into their calculations yet? No; only Anne has consciously wrestled with the issue at all. Will they begin to factor in marketplace considerations as they make their next writing choices? Probably not, since thinking about the marketplace is not uppermost in a writer's mind as she begins to wrestle with her material. We might hope and wish that our writers invent an exercise equivalent to the framing exercise presented in this chapter or in some other way think about angling their work toward potential readers. But this is rarely how a writer begins, consumed, as she usually is, with how to most effectively bring her thoughts and feelings to life.

Amelia's working title for her insane asylum book is the Jane Austen–like *Pain and Possibility*. Her way of working is to write whatever comes to mind, to write without censoring herself. This way of writing feels chaotic, wild, and even dangerous, but is also the most natural. When she reads the scene fragments she's producing—here a scene that is nothing but the description of a scream, there a scene that is nothing but a snapshot of the yellow walls of the asylum—she worries that she's producing a gigantic pile of puzzle pieces that she won't be able to fit together. But she shrugs that possibility away and continues to write on the wild side.

Marjorie's working title is *The Old Lady Dies*. She finds herself writing scene after scene between a mother and daughter, even though these scenes keep putting the murder off. She has the suspicion that she should step back and make an outline, plot the novel, refine her detective's character, spend time working on the setting—make some efforts at order. But for now she feels compelled to write intense, almost unbearably sad mother-and-daughter scenes, simultaneously letting neither character off the hook while preparing for the murder. Her choice, like Amelia's, is to go where she feels she must go—to just write.

Sam has made a different sort of choice. Out of fear that he has nothing to say and a belief that he'd better toe the line, he retreats from his commitment to examine his subject. He makes the decision to choose a simpler subject, one recommended by his thesis adviser. Sam commences a literature search and soon accumulates hundreds of synopses and citations. But he can feel his writer's block returning with a vengeance. After a few weeks he stops collecting data and tries to confront his own feelings. He doesn't like the choice he's made, to focus on his adviser's subject, but he can't seem to convince himself to return to his richer, riskier first choice. After a while he finds himself avoiding thinking about his thesis altogether.

Anne's choice, with which she is not entirely comfortable, is to write a book that is as commercial as she can make it without doing too much violence to her soul. She really wants a breakout book and a way off the publisher's midlist. But after weeks of holding this intention, she still doesn't know what she's supposed to be writing. The task is making her feel grumpy, blue, and a little insane, but she's determined to hold out for a bestseller idea. Her central choice is to not launch into an eloquent midlist book like the ones she's written many times before.

Unlike Anne, Henry is not looking to write a bestseller, although he'd take one if it came. His main decisions are to refrain from writing glibly and to reclaim his lost integrity. The working title for the book he's contemplating is *Everything You Ever Wanted to Know About Bisexuality: A Complete Guide to Loving Men and Women*. He knows that to promise to explain bisexuality when he doesn't understand it himself is not the epitome of honesty, but he takes a deep breath and reminds himself that he doesn't have to write it until he's ready.

Like our five writers, you have choices to make. The first is to choose to begin. If you haven't made that choice yet, please make it now. Also think about what I've been discussing in this chapter, about balancing the desire to write deeply and personally with the desire to gain an audience and succeed in the marketplace. It may take you a considerable while to know what you want to write or what your book is about, just as it's taken our five writers real time and effort to begin to understand their projects. But as you can tell, our writers aren't so far ahead of you that, with some steady jogging and a good sprint at the end, you can't catch up.

Honoring
the
Process

Honoring the process means, first of all, accepting the complexity of writing. I mean not paying lip service to but really accepting complexity. Who can blame us for wanting guarantees? Who can blame us for dreaming of not making mistakes? But a process is a process, and writing is no different; it is inherently intricate and often painful. If you want to write deeply you have to accept the fact that every piece of writing is a voyage into the unknown, a voyage hard on the navigator and full of potential disasters. It is possible to positively influence the writing process, but first you must accept the reality of that process.

Try the following experiment. Imagine that a good idea comes to a would-be writer. Imagine that this would-be writer doesn't jot down the idea but instead goes about his business of watching television, answering the phone, making a sandwich, and going to the gym to play racquetball. Will the idea still be there when he gets home from the gym? The odds must be one hundred to one against. The fact that he didn't rush to his desk to record his writing idea means that this writer is not trying to hold onto his own ideas; that he doesn't really care about them. If asked, he might say something like "I'd love to write, but I'm just not creative" or "I always got A's in English, but I never get any good ideas." He doesn't realize that he's refusing to do one of the most natural things it takes to be a writer: jotting down writing ideas when they come.

If there is meaning to the phrase "honoring the process," there must also be meaning to the phrase "dishonoring the process." The first makes no sense unless the second does also. I hope that you'll take seriously the notion that you can help or harm the writing process and that, in a corner of awareness, you already know which of the two you are doing. You won't have this awareness all the time or perfectly, and sometimes in good faith you'll plant a garlic bulb even though you're dreaming of tulips. But when you find the courage to explore your own truth about honoring and dishonoring the process, some writing successes are bound to happen.

Writing a Novel in Two Months' Time

The writing process is complex, not simple. To get from here to *The Brothers Karamazov* is not a walk in the park. Even if writing a given book were fast and effortless—as sometimes the writing of a book *is*—the personality and history of the human being doing the writing provide the complexity. The writer has thought, felt, and experienced a million things. If you are Dostoevsky, you've been nearly executed by the Czar; your tyrannical father was killed by his own servants; you are afflicted with some terrible malady, maybe epilepsy, maybe panic attacks. You've been imprisoned in Siberia. You were discovered by Russia's preeminent literary critic, to whom your roommate boldly hand-delivered the manuscript of your first novel. You started out radically liberal and ended up radically conservative. And, before you die, you write *The Brothers Karamazov*, whose very existence is testament to the fact that out of exactly this complexity of life, and not some idyll, comes deep writing.

The internal processes that precede writing are always anything but simple. A writer may complete her stage play in a weekend or her novel in three weeks, the amount of time it took the Belgian novelist Georges Simenon to write his novels. She may write her nonfiction book in six months or a year. But to imagine that the writing process has been limited to those few days, weeks, or months is to forget to include conception and gestation in one's definition of the birthing process. Birth is more than labor and delivery.

Take the case of the last novel I wrote, during the early part of 1997. Several years before that winter a certain idea had begun to pester me. I began to wonder why Israeli Jews stayed in the Middle East when peace there looked to be a patent impossibility. Why didn't the Jews of Israel pack up and create an equally "sacred" homeland somewhere else? This seemed like an excellent idea for a novel, both intellectually interesting and commercially viable.

I wanted the novel to make headlines, stir debate, and even spur Israel's move. This may sound grandiose and ridiculous, and of course I'm not saying it with a straight face. But I also am. How influential were books like *Uncle Tom's Cabin, The Silent Spring,* or the novels of Orwell or Solzhenitsyn? Maybe very influential. Who can say? I wanted *Moving Israel* to get Israel moving. I wanted to change the course of history.

After many hesitations and false starts, I wrote the novel. The actual writing took only two months, but all the preliminaries were as integral to the process of writing *Moving Israel* as the sixty active writing days in the winter of 1997. As it happened, although I'd never kept a journal in conjunction with my writing before and never have since, this time I did. These excerpts show how long and arduous the preliminaries can be.

April 15, 1994

Tax day. I'm about to begin on New Jerusalem *[my working title]. Yesterday the first sentence came to me:*

"A Jew can do anything," Lev Goldstein said, "except stem the tide of history."

Just a year ago I was certain that I would never write fiction again. Nonfiction was so much the better bet that for me to think about writing fiction felt like an act of bad faith, a piece of irresponsibility. I have children, a mortgage, retirement needs. If I stick to nonfiction I can perhaps build a career: maybe the odds are ten to one against me, or twenty to one. As a writer about artists' issues I am growing a reputation, and a real career as a nonfiction writer is not a dream but a near reality. But in fiction, the odds must still be a thousand to one against me, or worse. Why, then, write it?

Because this time I have a new goal. This time I mean to do commercial, plot-driven, market-wise fiction that, parenthetically, I can also be proud of.

But I have my doubts that I should try to do this. I won't begin it unless and until I believe in its commercial viability.

April 16, 1994

What I hoped wouldn't happen is happening. I'm writing the novel, despite my pledge not to start yet. I wrote two pages of dialogue between Lev and a newspaper editor because I saw Max Frankl, retiring executive editor of the New York Times, *on* Charlie Rose *today.*

April 17, 1994

Plot elements are coming to me unbidden.

Yesterday I taught at St. Mary's and was otherwise kept busy throughout the day. But still I stopped to record thoughts on the novel. Today the plot summary came to me:

A Jew sets out to move Israel to the South Pacific.

I've never before been able to say in a sentence what a novel of mine was about, partly because they weren't "high concept" or plot-driven books, partly because I refused to make the effort.

In this book I will do what an agent some years ago said I must do: "Reign in my quirkiness." I'll focus on telling a good story. I'll invent drama and not wait to see what drama wants to unfold. I'll "make something happen."

Yesterday and again today I told Ann that I might be writing a novel, even though I'd sworn that I wouldn't write fiction again. But I made it clear that I meant to write commercial fiction, that my goal wasn't to tell a wonderful psychological story but to sell. As always, she gave me her blessing. What if she were another sort of person? Then I couldn't have this life.

April 19, 1994
Sunday afternoon the support group I formed met for the second time. In March I told them that I only write nonfiction, that I would never write fiction again. I explained why. This meeting I told them about New Jerusalem. I gave them the plot in a sentence. They got it instantly, loved it, wanted to see it written. I could hear in the reactions of these not-babes-in-the-woods the kind of enthusiasm that could be generated at a publishing house.

April 20, 1994
I think what I'll do today is begin to plot New Jerusalem.

But how do you plot a novel? I have a master's degree in creative writing. I've written many novels, including three, written during my ghostwriting career, that were plot-driven (but not plotted out beforehand). I've read a lot of fiction. But for all that I can't say that I know how to plot, not the way that I can say that I know how to teach a class or counsel a client. How do you plot?

I want to write commercial fiction. But I do not know how to plot, which must mean that I do not want to plot. Is this my Waterloo?

April 21, 1994
I did some plotting yesterday. I can't say that it went well and I can't say that it went ill and I can't say that I feel anything but sour today.

October 28, 1994

Six months have passed. In those months, I wrote Fearless
Creating, *after I sold it to Jeremy Tarcher. Then I began obsess-
ing about a book about atheism—but working on it upset and
disoriented me, because each day my belief grew that no such
book would ever be wanted. So I stopped, and the moment I
stopped a "small" book came to me, a book of affirmations for
artists. I took a week and put together a proposal for it, and yesterday I mailed that to my agent.*

After I'd mailed the package, I began on New Jerusalem
*again. Now it seems it is somehow informed by the work I
did on atheism—by Thomas Paine, by Voltaire, by the obscure
Catholic priest who near death converted to atheism and
wrote a brilliant anti-Church manifesto that somehow got
into Voltaire's hands, by the British freethinker Chapman
Cohen, by the philosopher Anthony Flew, who wrote of the
"cold war of the mind" between believers and nonbelievers, by
Madalyn Murray O'Hair, who wrote interestingly on the idea
that one can't be both a Jew and an atheist, that Jews have to
choose.*

So New Jerusalem *is a different book now. But how?*

November 3, 1994

*I thought that the idea for this novel came to me just this year.
But this morning while looking for something on an old disk
dating back to the spring of 1991 I came across a file labeled*
NEWJEW.

A very strange thing.

I pulled up the file and read the first couple of sentences.
New Jerusalem.

The relocation of Israel to an island in the Pacific.

Why didn't I drop everything to write it back then? I can imagine why. First, I'd long before stopped believing in the possibility of selling literary fiction. Second, I had no confidence that I could write mainstream fiction, having previously failed at my half-hearted attempts. Third, this would have been early in my pledge never to write fiction again. Fourth, I had good ideas all the time and had stopped believing in the significance of good ideas.

But to have entirely and completely not remembered!

November 9, 1994

I've been working on the book steadily for five or six days, but I haven't noticed the time. On some days I go to a cafe and get an orange scone and coffee and write before picking the girls up from school. When did I last work on a novel in a cafe? It is absolutely the thing I am easiest with. Pad, pen, people passing, it is my heaven on earth.

November 15, 1994

It's raining hard. I see by my last entry that a week ago I was working well on the book. Not this past week. Why? Because, along with the strong desire to write it, I possess the equally strong desire to ignore it and punish it.

I wonder if I can explain this. The book and I are on friendly terms. (I haven't been on friendly terms with all the books I've written.) On certain days we are in love. But no novel will dictate to me again. "Never again!" I want this novel to understand its place in my life. So this past week I rejected it even on days when, all things considered, I might have worked on it. And in proving this point I've let some days slip by that, as I write this entry, I regret having squandered.

Friday the Thirteenth. Two months have passed since I wrote in this journal. I've been working intensely during this time on revisions of Fearless Creating. *I've thought about* New Jerusalem *virtually not at all, nor have I been thinking about any other book. I would have to say that* New Jerusalem *isn't tugging at me, even though a few weeks ago my friend Gary Camp sent me several pages of provocative quote material. His contributions helped me see the book more clearly. But despite that shot in the arm, the novel is not alive in me at this moment.*

Almost two years have passed since I wrote in this journal!

I spent 1995 and 1996 writing three books and most recently a proposal for a book on creativity issues in therapy. I must write that book next. But since the turn of the year I've felt compelled to return to the novel.

Am I really writing it this time? Or will I next encounter this journal in the year 2000?

I did write *Moving Israel* this time. Today it is with a literary agent who is looking to find it a publisher. I ended up writing it in sixty days, but I had it in mind for more than six years. Each of us is likely to experience such twists and turns, such starts and stops, as we take an idea or a feeling and internally "process" it. Let me predict how Amelia, Marjorie, Sam, Anne, and Henry will experience this writing process as they embark on their Wonderland journey to who-can-say-where.

Entangled in Process

Amelia is writing her madhouse novel. But because it isn't plot-driven, because she's not sure what she intends the book to be about, and because she doesn't know who the main character is (sometimes it seems to be an institutionalized young woman, sometimes it seems to be that character's sister, sometimes it seems to be a third woman trapped in the hospital's locked ward), she finds herself writing bits and pieces, part-scenes and single sentences, which do not go together in any discernible way.

Finally, tired of this road (which is winding exactly as it must wind, but how can she know that if she doesn't have a map, road signs, previous experience, or a clear destination?), Amelia decides that she *must* make some plot. Out of frustration, she decides that she will give her novel a plot line, and that she will do it today. She hammers out a plot having to do with a gay man, Lenny, a nurse in the locked ward, who did not exist yesterday. She writes for a month and ends up with a hundred pages. Then she reads what she's got. Parts of it are good, but overall she hates it. For the next two months she doesn't write anything.

Amelia is now "blocked." One solution to her problem, not the best, perhaps, but the one she's most likely to choose, is to decide to "just write the damned book" and see how it turns out. A second solution is for her to say, "Either I'll come up with some effective changes, not just revising the book but revisioning it, or, if that fails, I'll abandon this novel for now and move on to the next thing." Both are reasonable options. But right now, entangled in the process, in the throes of first novel pains, Amelia is not able to make one of these choices. A crisis is brewing within her, and she begins to wonder if she shouldn't move to Italy or pierce a body part.

Marjorie, because she's writing a detective novel, on the face of it has an easier road to negotiate. She knows that she must provide clues, a murder, a murderer, a female detective. She has no intention of writing a French absurdist mystery in which nothing actually happens. She's not embarking on a Czech mystery that doubles as an allegory about bureaucracies. She's writing a straightforward, sensible mystery, where rigor mortis sets in like clockwork. But she too is blocked.

Not totally. She writes little bits, then revises them and revises them. Out of a whole melon she gets a spoonful of fruit. In a corner of her awareness she knows that her critical tendency is *the* issue, making her hate her sentences and despise herself, but she can't seem to rein in her self-unfriendliness. Like Amelia, Marjorie doesn't understand how ugly and awful the first draft of a first novel can be. More than Amelia, Marjorie chastises herself for that ugliness. How could someone who's read so many books write something so awful? How could someone who's taken so many writing workshops still use the passive voice? How could she split infinitives here and let her characters say such inane things there? How could she be such an idiot?

Perhaps Marjorie should write her first draft all the way through, ugly as some sentences and scenes are bound to be. It might be best if she just wrote, letting in life and all the mistakes that gain entry, not stopping to revise until the killer daughter is arrested and the girl detective makes her last witty remark. But all Marjorie is doing right now, entangled in process and beset by doubts, is putting commas in and taking commas out. She is so assiduously fine-tuning her sentences that nothing alive is happening.

Sam, having retreated from the challenge of looking deeply into the subject of the emotional support of employees, isn't writing at all. If Amelia and Marjorie are blocked, Sam is neck-deep in concrete. He tells himself that writing is a game that he can't play, that writers are people who spout off self-indulgently, and that he, on the other hand, favors concision and precision. The world is filled with too much nonsense already, and he sees no reason to contribute more garbage. He says to himself that when the time comes he'll launch right into his dissertation, which should fly at that point since he'll be so ready.

However, if Sam thought back, he would recall that no dissertation topic ever came to him during that time period he spent not thinking about dissertation topics. He made the same arguments then that he is making now, about how ideas have to be incubated, about waiting patiently until the right idea comes along, about the value of getting right up to deadlines and using them for motivation. Out of fear and anxiety he's forgotten that he was going nowhere until he committed to hushing his mind, holding a writing intention, making a plan, and performing all those other steps that, for a brief moment, opened him up to good thinking.

Anne has had several good ideas come to her. From among them she's chosen one to work on. She's decided to write a novel about five young women who, after graduating from college, embark on a trip to Europe and witness a murder in Seville. Not having gotten a clear look at the murderer, they give their statements to the police, return home, and forget about the incident. They start their postcollege lives, each beginning an interesting job and connecting with a new boyfriend. Then one of the five turns up murdered. Has the killer followed them from Spain? It appears so. Is the killer one of their new boyfriends? That also seems likely.

Anne's intention is to write a plot-driven, character-driven novel in the "four women" tradition, a mainstream, bestseller novel full of romance and suspense. But she can't quite get started. The question is not who these women are or what the plot elements should be, though all of that is up in the air. The problem is more amorphous and more fundamental: the tone of the book. Anne seems to be writing either too lightly or too darkly, now one way and now the other. Her light writing sounds like a parody of bestseller fiction, and her dark writing sounds exactly like her customary voice, which she assumes can't be wanted in this sort of book.

She's reminded of something she once read about why good writers have trouble writing for the mass market. She finds the piece, a 1963 article by William Barrett called "Writers and Madness," and rereads the relevant passage.

It seems, after all, impossible to write a best-seller in complete parody: one has to believe in one's material even there, and it looks to be impossible to fake unless one is a fake. Writing is not so uncommitted an intellectual effort that a writer can drop down facilely to a very much lower level and operate with enough skill there to convince that kind of reader.

She's not sure if this is the truth or a rationalization. Is she really incapable of writing bestseller fiction, or is her pride just in the way? Or is it that if she could believe in her material in some new way she might be able to proceed? This feels to her like an insight. What exactly would this new way of believing be? Anne orients herself toward an answer to this question; she offers the answer a standing invitation. It has permission to come to her whether she is waking or sleeping, writing bills or doing the dishes. She really wants to learn about this new way of believing; and for the first time she feels optimistic about her chances of cracking the riddle of bestseller writing.

Henry is having a good time. Having peeked into the bisexuality literature, he's convinced that nothing too interesting has been attempted there yet. Much of the psychological writing is rehashed Freudianisms about "sadomasochistic inversions," ideas that feel shallow and biased to Henry. The sociologists writing on androgyny, a cousin of bisexuality, look to have an opposite ax to grind. For them, "being both" is the natural way. He sees that each side has its agenda, the one to pathologize bisexuality and the other to normalize it, but that neither is very close to understanding the reality of living, breathing bisexuals.

The writing he likes are interviews and biographies. He's fascinated by interviews with gay HIV+ artists in Andrea Voucher's *Muses from Chaos and Ash* and interviews with lady rock-and-rollers in Liz Evans's *Women, Sex, and Rock 'N' Roll*. Something is percolating in his brain as Henry reads. He's not sure if what he's thinking about has to do with bisexuality at all. But he knows that he feels alive and engaged.

His only problem is that he has no idea what he's doing. This is not a feeling that he's tolerated very well in the past. Invariably he'd rush to impose a shape on his unformed thoughts, launching quickly into a sexy comedy or a violent action drama. But this time he wills himself to hang out in "don't know," a place that feels weird, spacious, and inspiring.

Digging In

Deep writing requires process—the creative process, the writing process—nothing less and nothing else. Confusion on this score ruins the writing lives of millions of would-be writers. They think that the deep writer gets to the mountain top by flying up, whereas they, being plodders, are doomed to the flatlands. But we are all geniuses, and we are all plodders. You might say that if you have the bulb you have the tulip. But no—the bulb only has tulip potential. The actuality requires process.

The writing process can't be pinned down. It might take you sixteen years to write a certain poem, because of an elusive word. A word eluding you for that long is part of the process. You might write something excellent and then, unaccountably, follow that up with something stupid. Ups and down are part of the process. You might drag your characters to Iceland, because you visited there and want to describe its lava landscape, when the plot calls for them to go to Denmark. Mistakes are part of the process. You might write for six hours straight one day, but take the next day off to walk by the shore. Effort and relaxation are both part of the process.

A year ago you may have loved poetry that rhymes, and today you may hate it. Changing your mind is part of the process. Sometimes you may write calmly, like a Zen master sitting zazen, and sometimes you may write in a frenzy, driven by an idea that must be captured or lost. No one particular energy defines the process. You may be able to slough off a hundred criticisms, then take one deeply to heart and not write for years. Getting badly hurt is part of the process. You may avoid approaching a big publishing house because you feel too small or a small house because you feel too big; you may avoid the editor across the room because you feel self-conscious; you may avoid writing about what you love because that feels like cheating. Both not doing and doing are part of the process.

What honoring the process means is that you accept these ups and downs and natural difficulties without too much complaint. You work to influence the process in a positive way. You write. You keep an open heart. You keep an open mind. You reread and revise. You accept that certain pieces will not work, and you rejoice when pieces turn out well. You chastise and berate yourself only rarely, and you keep your eye on the writing at hand. You go deep and try to tell the truth. You dig in: you pull on your writing clothes, grab your favorite pen, and immerse yourself in the process.

Befriending
the
Work

Loving and befriending your work are principles second to none in the deep writer's life. As the artist Helene Aylon put it, "Because there is a fear of sentimentality, love is not very often addressed—and it is really the one motivation in all of our lives." Love is what the deep writer lavishes on her work. That's not to say that on a given day the work isn't roundly hated. It is, and on too many days! But the underlying relationship is still one of love.

In practice, it may be more useful to think about befriending your writing than loving it. To have a friend means to work at relationship. If you have a writing friend, you read her writing, help her get published, give her advice from the heart, and go to her booksignings. You notice her depressions and give her support, you listen when she complains about agents or editors, and you help her when she asks for help. That is friendship. Befriending your writing implies the same sort of relationship.

There is wisdom in thinking of your work as a friend and treating it like a partner, a dear adversary, an intimate, a colleague. To do so gives it a voice in the proceedings, so that when you say to yourself, "Boy, will I get even with my boss in the next paragraph!" the work has a way to respond. "Please don't do that," it says. "That's your agenda. It's doesn't help my narrative flow at all." Considering your work a friend allows you to enter into dialogue with it, you speaking your desires and it having the chance to counter, "Yes, yes, I know you love that shade of blue, but I'm a book about yellow, damn it!"

We do not have an intimate form of "you" in the English language, and we really need one. The work is a "tu." "Je t'aime," not "je vous aime." This addressing of your work as a "tu" is a threshold that would-be writers have a hard time crossing. It is like crossing over to self-acceptance or surrendering to self-love. It is the very opposite of unhealthy narcissism, where you demand of the world that it love your work whether it is good or bad. Rather it is you committing to your work and becoming its ally. The work requires your advocacy, kindness, compassion, and friendship. To be even firmer about it, it requires your love. How well do you love?

Totem Hugs

On the way to one of my writing workshops I'll stop to pick up some small, smooth stones from my garden, picking up as many stones as there are participants in the workshop. I choose the stones carefully; they are to serve as totems of friendship between the writers in the workshop and their work.

I'd like you to find such a totem object for yourself. It should be a small object that fits in the palm of your hand: smooth stones are excellent, but you might try a foreign coin, a gemstone, a clay ball you hand-form and fire yourself. When you find yourself blocked or in any difficulty with your work, try the following exercise. Get your totem. Frame the problem objectively first. This might sound like, "My detective is boring" or "I've digressed for the last ten thousand words." Instead of trying to solve the problem, speak to your work. Let it know that you and it are in this together. Always end by saying, "I love you, work." Then squeeze your totem, symbolically giving the work a hug.

Consider the following dozen problems that arise in the course of writing and the ways that you might join with your work in addressing them. Each time you address your work, remember to give it a hug.

1. How can I love my work when I hate it so damned much?

   "I don't hate you, work. I'm just sad that you're not all that you should be and that I haven't done an adequate job. I do love you, work."

2. How can I love my work when it frightens me to work on it?

   "I'm not afraid of you, work. We're friends, after all! I'm just afraid that I'll make mistakes and disappoint myself. I do love you, work."

3. How can I love my work when it's gone so far astray?

> "Dear work, we do have problems! I feel like we've wandered off the road into a ditch. Can we make it back? I do love you, work."

4. How can I love my work when I don't know what in God's name to do with it?

> "I am confused and lost, work, but I won't let confusion ruin our friendship. We'll find our way. I do love you, work."

5. How can I love my work when my life is so crazy?

> "The craziness is a terrible problem, work. But being with you is actually a place of sanity. I do love you, work."

6. How can I love my work when it feels so shallow and superficial?

> "I've done you a disservice, work! I must not have given you what you needed. Let's revise or even start over. I do love you, work."

7. How can I love my work when I can't even remember it?

> "I am a poor friend, work, to have forgotten all about you! But I mean to do better. I do love you, work."

8. How can I love my work when everyone else hates it?

> "Critics can't bother us, work, even the accurate ones, for no critic understands our relationship. I do love you, work."

9. How can I love this work when I should be doing some other piece?

> "What do you think, work? Should it be serial monogamy or multiple friendships? A good question! But whatever the answer, I do love you, work."

10. How can I love a work when it's lost all its momentum?

"We've slowed to a stop, you and I. Let's reignite and catch fire! I do love you, work."

11. How can I love this work when I've forgotten why I began it?

    "Must I know why I loved you then in order to love you now? I don't see why. I love you here and now. I do love you, work."

12. How can I love my work when thinking about it makes me feel depressed and defeated?

    "I do get depressed, work. That's the truth. I do sometimes despair. But it's not your fault, and I don't blame you. I do love you, work."

Entering into friendly relationship with our work means changing how we talk to ourselves and how we use our heart. Usually we say things to ourselves like "The book isn't going well" or "I have no idea how to end this chapter." We say these things with a cold heart and expect that our minds will provide us with some good solution. We forget or do not understand that with our work, as with a friend, problems often are best met with empathy, a kind word, and a hug. A new idea may be required in order to solve a problem—you may have to bring your character back from Alaska or insert a chapter on earth between the chapters on sky and water—but the process of arriving at that idea involves opening your heart as well as engaging your mind.

This approach may sound loony to you. Some folks who come to my workshops do snicker and sneer at the totem hug exercise. To be asked to hug smooth stones and chat with their book was not what they had in mind when they signed up. But they come around. The truth is undeniable: we do not feel enough, we do not put enough heart into our writing, we are not self-friendly enough or friendly enough with our work. A little hugging is required. A smooth stone clasped in your palm and squeezed to symbolize heartfelt connection can help. This is common sense, not lunacy.

Crafting Friendship

We left Amelia with about a hundred consecutive pages of her novel written. So far she's spent her time following Lenny, the gay male nurse who didn't figure in her original conception of the book, through a routine morning in the locked ward. Nothing much has happened yet. These early scenes have been primarily descriptive and consist of whole pages that investigate the quality of light filtering through barred windows, the texture of the plastered walls, the look of a woman doing a drug-induced shuffle.

According to Amelia's plot outline, Lenny is supposed to witness the brutal rape of the mad woman of the locked ward. But this just doesn't feel right to her. It isn't the story she intended to tell. While the rape scene will surely be filled with screams, they aren't the screams Amelia heard when the book first came to her. On the other hand, she wonders if she's supposed to go ahead and write scenes like these anyway, even when they don't feel right. Maybe this is the way first novels have to go. Even if it is, she can't make herself continue.

Stuck, she comes upon the totem hug exercise. The idea of befriending the work interests her, and she realizes that she doesn't feel at all friendly toward this novel. She decides to try the exercise. The right totem eludes her as she looks around her apartment, but the mention of smooth stones makes her think of a river upstate and how much she would love to get out of the city. In the past, when feeling blocked or confronted by a deadline, she has often fled to the country. This time she has a different idea: not to flee but to befriend her work by taking it on a "working vacation." Something about the phrase "working vacation" resonates for her. She packs up her novel-in-progress and heads for the country.

As she drives up to the river she's flooded with ideas. Several times she has to pull over to write down her thoughts. She sees that she is thinking about something new, something different, although she can't quite make out what this new book is about. She sees sunshine, not the shadows of locked wards. Someone is anorexic. There's a scene where a thin woman cooks a big meal and demands that everyone eat, while she herself pushes her food around on the plate. There's another scene in which this same woman tears a copy of *Glamour* to shreds. All this has nothing to do with the madhouse novel, at least not in any way she can fathom.

When she gets to the river she finds an evocative bend and parks along the shoulder of the road. She takes out her pad and the pages of the novel she's written so far, even though carrying them makes her feel self-conscious, and climbs down to the bank. She tries to sit and write, but she finds that she's got too much going on inside of her. She has to get up and take a brisk walk. She knows that she's on the verge of something: maybe it's the madhouse novel reshaping itself, or maybe it's something entirely different. Whatever it is, it's building up and getting ready to burst forth.

Then, just like that, a new plot, new characters, and a new

setting come to her. She sits down and writes. In this new novel, two young fashion magazine editors—Carla, the protagonist, and her rival and lover, who has no name yet—inflict pain on each other as they compete at the magazine and in life. The editor with no name finally cracks, a breakdown that Carla precipitates. Carla visits her lover at the hospital and they scream together, like wild animals howling in grief. The title of the novel comes to Amelia: *Eggshell White*. That turns out to be the color of the asylum's common room, and it also has something to do with the way that such women sometimes break.

Amelia loves the screaming scene. Thinking about it sends chills up and down her spine. She wants to write that scene, to hear Carla and her lover scream together. The novel's opening paragraph comes to her.

> *The thinnest women in the world worked at* Beautiful Girl, *the magazine for women who called themselves girls. But Carla was even thinner, even taller, even paler than they, which made her arrival that Tuesday morning a breath-catcher. By noon she'd received half a dozen invitations for lunch from assistant editors like herself who wanted to see how she handled not eating in public. Would she order big and move her food around? Would she order small? These were the things about Carla that one needed to know. The consensus was that she'd drink her lunch and not even bother pretending to eat.*

Amelia rereads the paragraph and has the sure feeling that she's on to something. This will be a book about rivalry, lust, love, pain, and fear—all the things she always knew it would be about. Now she has the setting, the characters, the story, the tension, everything. Sitting by the river she writes quickly, as if taking dictation. She understands where she is going and how she will get there. She has managed to avoid spending a year or two writing the wrong novel, and this lucky break came about because she befriended the work. She took her work on vacation, as opposed to taking a vacation from her work.

When we left Marjorie, she, too, had blocked. She'd started out with enthusiasm and freedom, writing one vitriolic mother-daughter scene after another, but then she'd begun microscopically revising those scenes instead of plunging ahead. Now, rather than honoring the process and entering into right relationship with her work, she's fallen into a depression, which she tries to lessen by taking an occasional mystery-writing workshop. But she can see that she's in despair and that she's taking her despair out on everyone around her.

Then she has a bit of luck. She learns of a writing group made up of four women and decides to visit it. Her luck is three-fold: that she's written enough on this novel that she feels entitled to join a group, that she is open-minded enough to make use of a writing group, and, luckiest of all, that it is a good group, loving, tough, and respectful. It is made up of writers who intend to write and publish and who aren't using the group as therapy, a social club, or a place for hand-to-hand psychological combat.

Actually, Marjorie's luck is fourfold: she is lucky that the group decides to admit her. Her first night is an audition that she almost bungles. She gets off to a good start by bringing a portion of her novel and agreeing to read from it. But then, as she's about to begin, she can't stop herself from apologizing for what she's written. One of the women gently informs Marjorie of a group rule: they don't apologize before or after reading. Intellectually, Marjorie understands the value of such a rule, but she finds it unbearably hard not to apologize. In fact, when she's done reading she blurts out a second apology. Someone reminds her of the rule.

It isn't her apologizing, though, that threatens her group membership—it's the way she responds to what the other women read. Despite her intuition that she should tone down her abrasive criticality, she doesn't. She says the first piece is awfully well written but "too complicated and obscure." She says the second piece feels overly simple and marketplace-driven. Her comments are intelligent and defensible but also unfriendly. Marjorie sees that these women, reacting to her "feedback," are not happy. All of a sudden she hears herself confessing, "I'm saying the wrong things. I'm sorry. I don't think I know how to be helpful and respectful. Please give me another chance!" After a long silence one of the women replies, "Just try to be on our side a little more. Remember how hard it is for all of us." All of a sudden Marjorie sees that befriending one's work is not the same as "being easy" on it. She has an epiphany. When the last person reads and it's Marjorie's turn to respond, she breaks down and cries a little. She doesn't know what to say. All she can think of is, "Thank you." That "thank you" gets her an invitation to join the group.

By the fifth or sixth meeting she can sense that her attitude toward her novel has changed. Now it is her intention to like it and help it, rather than hate it and kill it. She consciously works on stopping herself from calling it names, reproaching it, giving it a mental licking. When she's asked how the novel's going, she still has terrible trouble not crying out, "Just rotten!" But these days what she manages to say is "It's progressing nicely," a phrase with magic to it.

A month later she finds that she's stopped thinking of her book as a "dirty little secret." She tells her husband and then her mother about it. Her husband's reaction is positive, and her mother's reaction is negative, but she takes them both in stride. Instead of armoring herself with false pride, she begins to take genuine pride in the work, especially on those days when she likes what she's written. Such days come more often. Her mantras become "Forward!" and "No revising!" and "What happens next?" Some nights she dreams about the book; some mornings she wakes up and starts right in writing. She's wanted to spend more time with her mystery than with any friend.

Sam has gotten some help. With one deadline past and an extended date looming, Sam approached one of his committee members and asked him for a second extension. The professor agreed but suggested that Sam get outside help from a consultant.

In his first session with the consultant Sam is helped to see that he needs to choose between his first, deep idea, the emotional support of employees, and his second, strategic idea. In order to choose, he needs to reexamine his first idea with energy and enthusiasm. Sam is advised to spend the next day generating a list of dissertation topics related to the idea of employees and emotional support and to determine the pros and cons of each topic: which would be the hardest, which the easiest, which the most interesting, which the least interesting, which more favored by his committee members, which less favored, and so on.

The consultant asks Sam to fax him the list of evaluated topics. Nothing comes for four days. On the fifth day a brief fax appears, explaining that the list is not quite ready. Four days later, at midnight, the consultant gets the faxed list. He reviews it and calls Sam up the next morning. One of the consultant's goals is to model the decision-making process for Sam. Toward that end, he says, "Lots of these look good, but I think the first one is the richest, the fourth is the easiest, and the sixth is the one most likely to be accepted. What do you think?"

After a long pause Sam replies, "That sounds about right."

"Then think about what I've just said and choose a topic by our next meeting. All right?"

"Choose?" Sam says. "But how?"

"Just try."

At their next meeting, the consultant and Sam have the following conversation.

"Well, congratulations! You've chosen this one? 'Of the many components that constitute emotional support for employees, respect is the most important one. Those organizations that provide a culture of respect will see tangible bottom-line results and intangible workplace benefits.' "

"I think so. Maybe."

"All right. Next you need to get a full proposal ready to show your committee. How long will that take?"

"I don't know."

"What are the tasks? Enumerate them for me."

"I need to articulate the hypothesis—"

"Isn't that done already?"

"I guess so. I'd like to fine-tune it—"

"I'm not sure what you mean by 'fine-tune it.' Give me an example."

"I don't know. I'm choosing 'respect' to examine, but maybe I should go with something that's more easily observed or that can be operationally defined more easily—"

"So when you say 'fine-tune it,' you actually mean 'change it' for one reason or another?"

"I guess so."

"For what reasons?"

"I don't know. To make it clearer? More doable?"

"But we've agreed that it seems strong right now?"

"Yes."

"Then you have to be careful about trying to 'perfect' this. Liking it is more important than perfecting it. Do you like it?"

"What an idea! No, maybe I actually do. I think we haven't given 'respect' its due at all."

"Then get behind it. Be an advocate for this hypothesis!"

Over the course of some weeks and several "tough love" meetings with the consultant, Sam begins to realize that in order to write this dissertation he will have to not only make decisions but also, just as important, befriend his hypothesis. He sees that he is confronting something in himself that he's called indecisiveness in the past but that has more to do with loving the work he's undertaking and loving himself better. The consultant's idea of advocating for the hypothesis because it's worthy and likable has struck a chord and helps Sam move forward.

Anne has remained open to the idea that if she can get herself in right relationship to the book she's about to write, she'll be able to write it. But what right relationship actually means keeps eluding her. Then, one Saturday morning while doing the dishes, she has the oddest realization. She suddenly realizes that "joy" is part of "enjoy." From that linguistic observation she segues to the idea of "a woman enjoying herself." She sees this young woman in her mind's eye, a woman full of life who is about to embark on an exciting adventure. What adventure? The answer comes to her in an instant.

The young woman character is an independent filmmaker named Celeste whose award-winning work has come to the attention of a famous director. He invites her to participate in the making of his next film as an equal collaborator. Anne goes to the computer and writes the opening twelve pages of this book—which, just like that, she calls *Shooting Star*. When she reads what she's written, she sees that it is perfect bestseller fiction. How odd! The main character is lively, spunky, beautiful, and engaging. She is some sort of idealization, but she is also very human.

Anne sees that what she is doing is befriending this young woman, whom she flat-out likes. She is looking forward to the crises and adventures that are about to come Celeste's way, that are bound to come her way because of the situations into which Anne will drop her. Anne might have written a cynical novel about Hollywood, a satirical novel about publicity and the media, or something dark and moody set in the Los Angeles canyons, and such a book would have felt quite congenial to write. But this work, too, feels congenial, because it's connected to an exuberance and passion that also reside in Anne's heart.

Celeste is going to "make it," whatever that means in the

context of this novel. The prospect of a happy ending is already making Anne happy. Anne lets go of her novel about the five women who travel to Italy and witness a murder, a novel that had never really gotten started, and turns her attention to Celeste, who feels like a dear friend already.

Henry has been enjoying himself, reading widely, taking notes, and musing about what he's reading. He feels at once on vacation and as intellectually stimulated as he's ever felt. It doesn't matter to him whether he concludes that bisexuality is a sickness or a natural difference, a sin or a genetic predisposition. He's loving getting an education. Everything he reads, even material he hates, he loves, because it is all contributing to this education. Then one morning he writes the following.

> *Why am I bisexual? I don't think I'm going to learn the answer. That surprises me. I thought that I'd be able to solve this riddle if I did enough reading. Now I don't think so. The place where "sexual orientation" resides feels so deep that it may be inaccessible. If that's true, then I have to wonder who'll ever be able to explain why one child becomes this sort of person and another child that one.*
>
> *But I don't want to be prevented from investigating this question by the fact that it's unanswerable. So . . . maybe I'll write a memoir, but an odd memoir . . . a truthful recounting of my experiences, but interlaced with some good thinking about the abstract ideas I've been examining. I want to write something honest about my life, about the pain I've caused and why I caused it, about how loving men means something dif-*

ferent from loving women and what those differences are about. But I'd like to tie that to other things, to depression, mania, compulsions, obsessions. A nice little task! But that's what I feel like doing.

This morning, Henry feels ready to reveal himself and ready to befriend not so much the work as life itself.

On the Road to Loving

In my creativity consulting practice I work with clients on all aspects of the creative life: blocks, performance anxiety, depression, addictions, career choices, marketplace interactions, and so on. But the lion's share of the work always has to do with improving a client's self-relationship. Befriending the work and befriending the self are two faces of the same coin. One of my clients, provided these thoughts on growing this better self-relationship:

The creative journey is the never-ending process of giving birth to who we are. However we choose to share that with the world—through our painting, pottery, or poetry—the task of birthing ourselves is always arduous. So it made sense to me to find a midwife, someone who could support my unfolding and help me stay out of my own way. I wasn't interested in rummaging around in the psychodynamics of my past and my childhood—I wanted to pierce the present and begin to uncover the current personality of my creative process.

Like most garden-variety humans, I had a lot to learn about this. Generally, I'm much more familiar with the habit of bumping into myself and wrestling with all the goblins of self-limitation that have a particular appetite for eating away my confidence to create. To explore the mystery and challenge of this terrain, I wanted to work with someone who specialized in creativity issues; specifically, with someone who could help illuminate my version of "creator's block."

For years I'd been chewing on the question: "Where am I now creatively?" I would always experience the same response: a deep longing to share myself through writing and a simultaneous impulse to contain the expression of that. One part of me was dying to boldly sing its song, yet someone else inside—whose voice was louder—was paralyzed by an unknown fear. I felt trapped and frustrated, internally imprisoned by a force that denied me access to my creative resources.

In one of our first meetings, I remember showing Eric a graphic illustration of a particular inner process of mine that I wanted to write about. This picture was drawn on a big piece of butcher paper and depicted some of my favorite sub-personalities interacting with one another. Although I felt somewhat timid sharing such interior privacies, I was also excited that an important piece of me was being respectfully witnessed. In that moment, a delicate creative esteem grew a little stronger, and, to my surprise, the seed of a book was born out of that session.

One of the most powerful gifts of learning to write deeply has been the way it has helped me deepen my understanding of my inner shadow-creature, and therefore my encounter with the question: "What stops me from creating?" The answer, dressed in infinite costumes, is always the same. It is fear, fear like an octopus that, whenever you get too close to it, clouds the water *with black ink. But in those moments when I can take heart and keep looking until the ink clears, all I discover is a huge, joyous space waiting to be filled with life.*

Befriending your work is not so different from raising a child. The parent who possesses self-love and self-respect showers love and respect on his child. These magnificent gifts benefit the child as no other gifts can. Rather than attempting to master and dictate, the parent liberates the child, becoming that special friend, the one who cares the most. In the same way, the deep writer refuses to tame the work but instead acts as adviser, advocate, partner, friend, and lover. This is what the work requires. This is what the work deserves.

Evaluating
the
Work

Creation and evaluation each require a distinct awareness, and it is rare for anyone to do both well or often. The great writer is rare and the great editor is rare, and to find both in the same person is rarer still.

Some people evaluate brilliantly but do not create. They critique movies but do not make movies, dissect theories but do not produce theories, teach history but do not make history. Other people create lovingly and bountifully but do not evaluate enough. They paint fire but do not see when ice is wanted. They write with both eyes open but revise with one eye shut. They are struck by an elegant but bad idea and work it passionately, not noticing that the center isn't quite holding.

You must appraise your work in order to make sure that it is well built, well seasoned, well made. You befriend it, but you also judge it. You befriend the work and call it "thou," in order to write it, but you appraise it and call it "it," in order to make it right. You need to know whether the first half of your book is strong and the second half weaker. The deep writer does herself a disservice if she minimizes the place of evaluation in the writing process.

How do we decide if our writing is "working"? This sounds like an easy question to answer. We read what we've written and then we make a judgment: we like it or we don't. It has grammatical errors or it hasn't. It gets us from here to there or it doesn't. Sensible topic sentences introduce right-sized paragraphs; paragraphs line up and salute; chapters march together and count cadence; the book has the beginning, middle, and end that it should have; and we are done with it. What could be simpler? We read what we've written and say "Yeah!" or "Yuch!"

But evaluating writing isn't simple *at all*. Why? Because writing is nothing but argument and idea—whether the writing in question is a limerick, a fairy tale, a screenplay, or a training manual—and ideas and arguments are notoriously hard to evaluate. How do you decide whether Plato or Aristotle had the better ideas? How do you decide which are the best arguments for the existence of God and which are the best arguments against? These are the sorts of issues that confront writers, who are always arguing for one thing or another. If they are writing in favor of homeopathy, they are hoping to sway you in one direction, and if they are writing against homeopathy, they are trying to communicate different ideas and make a different case. If they set their novel on a beautiful, disease-free South Seas island, they are communicating one idea, and if they set their novel on an island of hurricanes, typhoid, and petty grievances, they are communicating another. A person can't string words together meaningfully without having ideas, because you can't get any word to follow any other word except for a reason.

It turns out that no book deals in facts. Think of the phone book. What could look more factual? But why are the Wangs grouped together and the Cohens grouped together? Because human beings have come up with the idea of alphabetical order. Why does AAA Shoe Repair come before Heart and Soul Shoe Repair? Because one firm has one idea about how to name itself and another firm quite a different idea. Why are county services separated from state services when their offices are in the same building? Why are people who do not want to be listed in the directory allowed that freedom? The answer is always the same: because we impose ideas on reality. Like every other piece of writing, a phone book is a constructed reality.

Take a familiar phrase like "A rose is a rose is a rose," which is chock full of ideas and arguments. If you tried to look at it any other way it would sound ridiculous and sophomoric. If you try your own version of the phrase—say, "A cow is a cow is a cow" or "A banker is a banker is a banker"—you'll have added a new idea, that you are making use of a well-known phrase for some particular reason, and that new idea, coupled with the ideas already embedded in the original phrase (about tautology, idealism, empiricism, and more) might or might not work. You or your editor might read your phrase and exclaim, "Trite!" But its problem is not that it's trite. Its problem, if it has one, is that you've mixed ideas and produced a new idea that must stand on its own merits.

Ideas work or they don't work; as to how or why they work, that is a very big subject! They work because they are ideas the reader wants. They work because they tickle the mind. They work because they fulfill a wish we have. They work because they connect in resonant ways, so that the idea of "molecule" and the idea of "machine" produce, when combined in a book like *The Engines of Creation,* the new idea of nanotechnology. There are probably 2,003 or 4,009 ideas in a novel like Kafka's *The Trial* alone.

Ideas are everywhere, in the words and, so to speak, behind the words, present because they are literally present and present even if they appear to be absent. A writer may despise the idea of zoos and communicate that hatred by writing a book about animals in the bush, never mentioning zoos, never alluding to zoos or dropping a hint about zoos. Because of the way the mind works, we get the message. There may be no white people in a book set in an imaginary black community, and that may be because the writer wants to say something about whites. We get that message, too. A book about the ethical nature of Christ may in fact be an argument against Christ's divinity. A book of recipes for winter soups made by cloistered monks may really be an argument against the modern world. A book about small towns in Arizona may be the author's unconscious argument for early retirement. If you picture a page of writing as three-dimensional, with the words hovering a half-inch or so above the paper, then you begin to see where the ideas are: behind the words, between the words, really everywhere.

An effective minor character is a well-made bundle of ideas, and an effective major character is a well-made bundle of ideas to whom we are asked to pay more attention. The two characters are connected at the level of idea, and their plots do not even have to intersect for us to understand how one relates to the other. When a character does something "out of character"—because the plot makes an unfortunate demand, or because the writer has forgotten who the character is—we no longer find the argument convincing. We are not convinced that Mary could kill John; we are certain that she was fated to commit suicide.

Each piece of writing has its own logic. What are you trying to do in the piece you're writing? Take Shaw's play *Pygmalion* and *My Fair Lady,* the musical based on it. Each attempts a different thing, and each succeeds on its own terms. In *Pygmalion,* we learn that a repressed, arrogant, misogynist, class-conscious professor like Henry Higgins could never love Eliza Doolittle or any other woman. Taking the same basic story line, *My Fair Lady* tells a fairy tale that works in its own right, satisfying our wish to believe in mythic love, good luck, personal success, and happy endings. To evaluate means, first, knowing what sort of argument you want to present.

Second, evaluation means identifying the strengths and weakness of one's arguments. To say that a piece of writing is well made and fully realized is the same as saying that it is a strong, seamless argument. Have I said things that don't fit and that detract from my argument? Have I made too many arguments or contradicted myself? Have I confused the reader through illogic? Have I supported my arguments in the best way possible? The writer's task is to present clear ideas in a rhetorically powerful way: if I support my ideas well and you support your ideas well, then each of us will produce a good piece of writing, even if our ideas are diametrically opposed.

Willing Ourselves to Evaluate

How do we evaluate our work? Consider the following.

If you wanted to evaluate whether a certain alcohol treatment facility was right for you or a loved one, you would want to know what it costs, whether it accepts insurance, how effective its treatment methods are, what those methods are, the length of stay, the credentials of the providers, the human warmth of the providers and their life experience, the ratio of providers to patients, the facility's reputation, the facility's location, the amount and quality of aftercare, the extent to which family members are included or excluded, the proximity to home, the demographics of the patients, and several other things. These are your criteria of evaluation or "questions that need answering."

Once you had your answers, though, you would still have to make a judgment based on the meaningfulness of the information *to you*. Facility A might have the lowest recidivism rate and therefore might best meet the basic definition of "effectiveness," but to go there you would have to take out a second mortgage and endure six months of in-patient care. The very way I use the word "endure" in framing what in-patient care will feel like means that, in this hypothetical example, the length of stay will prove a vitally important criterion, maybe the most important. While there are objective things to learn in evaluating anything, what one does with that information is always subjective. All meaning is personal and idiosyncratic.

Because this evaluation process is arduous, we most often end up picking a facility based on the size of its Yellow Pages ad or the production values of its brochure. This is what we human beings do. We avoid evaluating because evaluation is hard work and makes us feel anxious. Thus the very first step in the evaluation process is to find the willingness to evaluate.

This is especially true when it comes to evaluating our writing. It is hard to find the willingness to look our own work in the eye. There are many reasons: we have our dreams and worthiness invested in the writing, we hate to see its flaws and problems, we know that what we learn may cost us weeks and months of new work, we fear that our ideas may turn out to be in conflict or our arguments weak. It pains us to see that our writing isn't working, and it upsets us to realize that more work is needed.

But you can't do the good writing you want to do if you won't evaluate your work. Recently an award-winning short story writer came in for a session with me hoping to unblock. She'd been working on her first novel for about two years but then had stopped writing. She hadn't been able to touch the novel for several months running. I had her tell me about the novel, and I interrupted her whenever I had questions to ask. She explained that the book was about two characters, A and B, but to my ear it sounded like the book's ideas resided in the relationship between A and another character, C. But A and C couldn't interact in this novel. The story line and shape of the novel prevented them from achieving any intimacy.

I brought this matter up, delicately but directly. I asked her questions, which she tried to answer, and she asked me questions, which I tried to answer. She thought about what I said. Finally she responded that she was of two minds. She couldn't help but feel that there was value in the novel as currently framed. But she owned that I might be on to something. I wondered aloud about the possibility of her abandoning the current novel in favor of a new one, in which A and C got to tell their story. She said that she would think about it. When we met a month later, she reported that our first session had been very painful but also very helpful. Between it and the second session she had jettisoned the old novel and begun a new novel, a great deal of which was already written. She was writing every day with enthusiasm and she felt on track again.

This is an example of evaluation. It caused the writer pain, but it was still what was wanted and needed. While it might be nice to engage in this process with another person—a friend, a writing buddy, a consultant, or one's editor—most of the time we have to do this work ourselves, all alone, experiencing pain when we learn hard truths and experiencing exhilaration (and some new anxiety) when we discover how to proceed. All writers have serious questions to ask and answer about their own work, and most of the time they must serve as their own editors and evaluators.

Funny Mirrors

I recommend the following special way of evaluating your work. It can feel strange at first, because it involves a process that is intuitive and impressionistic, but once you master it you can learn what you need to know about your writing in almost an instant. I call this process funny mirrors.

Imagine that you've taken your work to a surrealist amusement park, and you discover a funhouse there. You go inside and encounter a long corridor lined with mirrors on both sides. On one side are mirrors with names: the mirror of the adjective, the mirror of the original idea, the mirror of the living thing, and so on. On the other side are mirrors that have a place on them for you to inscribe your own names: the mirror of Editor Jane, the mirror of the German-American reader, the mirror of the subplot, and so on.

When you hold up your work to one of these mirrors, you see only and exactly what that mirror reflects. In the first mirror you might encounter a talking head, in the second an image or a scene, in the third a phrase written out in script. Sometimes nothing will appear, a nothing full of information, as when you hold up your work to the marketplace mirror and the mirror can find nothing in your work with commercial appeal. Sometimes there are question marks, exclamation points, or strange squiggles in need of deciphering. This is a surrealistic funhouse, after all, and sometimes what you see will need interpreting.

The following are the named mirrors:

- The Mirror of the Adjective
  When you hold your work up to this mirror, you get back a single word: dark, confused, rushed, sentimental, stiff, clever, simplistic, elegant, unflinching, detached, depressing, deep, commercial. This is the mirror's understanding—that is, your intuitive understanding—of your work's current state, summed up in a single word.
- The Mirror of the Original Idea
  Your piece of writing started somewhere, with a feeling, an image, an idea. This mirror will reflect back to you insights about whether and to what extent the work is still harboring that original idea and is still guided by it.

You might see a tiny dot: all that remains of your original idea. You might see an abstract painting: the idea gone wild, fragmented and mutated in the writing.

- The Mirror of the Living Thing

  In this mirror you get a sense of your work's organic growth: whether it is growing tall and spidery, short and squat, wild and unruly, spare and anemic. It may have nothing of the original idea left in it, but it may still be a healthy, thriving organism, growing with its own fine logic.

- The Mirror of Alternatives

  In this mirror you get a snapshot of how your work might look if written differently. This mirror is invaluable: you get to see powerful alternatives that may have eluded your vision because of your focus on the work-as-it-is. Each time you hold up the work you see another alternative: how the book might look if narrated omnisciently, or if Sally told the story instead of Harry, or if Sally's best friend did the telling.

- The Mirror of Shape and Form

  Every piece of writing has its own shape, its own architecture. In this mirror you might see reflected a skyscraper with the top fifty stories separated from the bottom fifty by a jarring gap of open air. Your book may be missing the middle chapter that connects the first half with the second. You might see a Calder mobile, which reminds you that the twittering bird chapter early on needs balancing with a meditation on the lightness of being.

- The Mirror of the Ideal Reader
  In this mirror a face appears and chats with you. He or she is serious, respectful, intimate, and understands your intentions but also has his or her own ideas about what is or isn't working. If you hold your work up a second time, a different ideal reader may appear, one with a different history and different tastes but one still absolutely on your side and interested in seeing your work succeed.

Here are ten more mirrors:

- The Mirror of the Typical Reader
- The Mirror of Narrative Flow
- The Mirror of Rhetorical Power
- The Mirror of Intention
- The Mirror of Voice
- The Marketplace Mirror
- The Mirror of Mystery
- The Mirror of Grandeur
- The Mirror of Truth
- The Mirror of Goodness

Can you imagine how each of these mirrors works? What do you see reflected in each of them?

When you want to know something in addition to the information available in the named mirrors, walk down the other side of the corridor. There stand the mirrors waiting to be named by you. You might hold your work up to a mirror you call Mary and get a short, important answer about whether

Mary is an effective character or a distraction. You might hold your work up to a mirror you call Dialogue and learn that your character John is making boring speeches and that Howard is barely grunting. You might hold the work up to a mirror you call Ending and learn whether your whisper of an ending is necessary, a problem, or both.

When you're working with an editor, then naturally you will want to add an Editor mirror to your funhouse array. When you hold your work up to this mirror you get to hear your editor's thoughts about the book. Editor Jane appears and says, "Darn it, boy, didn't we discuss this? I wanted much more action and much less philosophizing!" With this mirror you foretell editorial objections and nip problems in the bud by engaging in dialogue with your intuition. This mirror alone is worth the price of admission.

Visit this funhouse when you want to evaluate your work. Use exactly as many mirrors as you need. Invent the ones that will help you the most, creating custom-tailored mirrors that answer your most pressing questions. Have you written several short stories and wonder if they amount to a collection? Invent a mirror. Is your self-help book helpful enough? Invent a mirror. See what there is to be seen.

Listening to Warning Bells

You write a sentence and have the bad feeling that it's just sent the book in a wrong direction. But has it really? You introduce a character and have the sense that you are introducing her because she is odd and interesting, not because the book demands her. But is that true? Our "warning bell" sense serves many purposes, including alerting us to the fact that we've made a mistake, marking anxiety, signaling a critical but correct decision, and announcing that we're going deeper than we had anticipated going. We can't possibly turn on a dime every time we have a funny feeling about our work, and so it follows that only some warning bells should cause us to stop and take heed. But which are which?

I think a lifetime of writing helps us know, even though I've made so many mistakes in this regard, both recently and right to this minute, that thirty years of writing does not look to be long enough to figure it out. There may be no sure answer to the dilemma of knowing which warning bells to heed and which to ignore, but what can be learned is how to fashion a better relationship to these warning bells, so that even if one doesn't make perfect use of them—even if one fails to heed an emergency warning or comes to a full stop when only anxiety is present—one at least hears them clearly and gets to decide whether to stop or to proceed. To this day, I do not always stop when I should, but I do think I've acquired a better ear for the timbre and meaning of warning bells.

Consider our five writers. All five have been writing, which is splendid. While writing, they've had to evaluate at every turn, heeding some warning bells, ignoring others, and making countless good and bad choices. Now each has been halted by a warning bell so loud and insistent that writing through it is proving impossible. Each has been forced to come to a full stop. In the unlucky writer who doesn't realize that this crisis is just an evaluation moment and not a failure or a defeat, this forced halt would become a full-blown block. The work would get put away for six months or a year or abandoned forever. But our writers, working the program I'm outlining, understand that it is time to evaluate their work and not flee from it or castigate themselves.

Amelia, you will remember, abandoned her madhouse novel in favor of a novel set in a hip magazine office, where she is getting the chance to explore her themes through two characters, Carla, the protagonist, and Gwen, her officemate, rival, and lover. This setup still pleases her. But after writing some excellent, fast-paced scenes full of good language and incident, she finds herself blocked.

Amelia enters the funhouse and finds herself most attracted to the side of the corridor where the mirrors have no names. She names one mirror Carla and learns that Carla is violently alive, full of the wildness, goodness, badness, and startling contradictions that Amelia feels inside of herself. She moves on, naming the next mirror Gwen, and waits for something to happen. Nothing does. She knows that she can visualize Gwen, but the mirror is acting as if Gwen doesn't exist. Finally Amelia gets the picture. She hears herself admit, "I am not doing Gwen justice."

It comes to her that she must write a scene in which Gwen takes center stage, a scene in which Carla doesn't appear at all. As soon as Amelia says this to herself, a scene comes to her: Gwen visits her parents. It is a scene filled with no searing drama, only with a horrible coldness and absence of love. She writes this scene in no time, and it comes out as well as any scene so far. Not only does it help explain Gwen to the reader, it helps explain Gwen to Amelia. She suddenly sees where the plot must go — toward the madhouse, as before, but with a new twist and a new outcome.

Something big is bothering Marjorie, and she can even name the problem. Her mystery is no mystery. She has argued from the beginning, through scene after scene, that the daughter will kill the mother, and the daughter does. The reader knows this early and well. So, if this isn't a mystery, it must be some other kind of genre piece. Is it a police procedural, where her lady detective and a cop team up? Is it a suspense novel, where the killer is identified early and the plot centers around the hunt? The time is coming when all introductions must wind to an end and *The Old Lady Dies* must define itself.

Marjorie senses that she doesn't want to write a chase novel in which her detective knows the killer's identity and, always one step behind, chases her from locale to locale. Nor does she want to write a suspense novel in which the killer turns on the detective and begins to stalk her. The daughter has killed her mother for certain reasons, but she is not someone who would stalk her pursuers. What, then, will the novel be about? Rather than visit the funhouse, Marjorie takes her question to her writing group. She asks the members point-blank, "Here's where I'm stuck. What should I do?"

One member suggests that Marjorie drop most of her early scenes, so that the reader isn't so sure who the murderer is and the book becomes a traditional mystery. A second member has the idea of making the murderer someone else, of having all the clues, psychological and otherwise, point to the daughter, but having the murder really arise out of a love triangle. The third member suggests that the book be primarily about the lady detective, not the daughter and mother, and that it introduce the detective in such detail and with such panache that she becomes worthy of a series. The fourth group member suggests that, despite all the work it would entail, what's needed are several other suspects, maybe as many as three or four, each of whom has good reasons to kill the mother.

These suggestions combine and resonate with Marjorie and, as she thinks things over the next day, begin to feel shockingly liberating. She has focused so narrowly on the mother and daughter that she herself has had a claustrophobic reaction to the book. Because of the book's narrow focus, her own detective has had no way into the story, even though she's an interesting, likable character. Now Marjorie sees that in order to get the right voice, point of view, focus, and narrative flow going, she will have to invent other suspects and let go of many of the scenes between daughter and mother that she has already written. Her job is to turn the book into a traditional mystery. Having finally said that to herself, she finds herself ready to consider the book's architecture.

Sam has found himself blocked and stalled at every turn. Now, after many months of teeth-pulling, with his proposal accepted by his committee and his literature search done, he finds himself unable to put together the questionnaire that the subjects he recruits will be asked to complete. Each survey question he crafts looks lame, ambiguous, or misleading. After two weeks of doing no work on the questions, he makes an appointment to see his consultant—his hired mirror.

"What's the next thing that's required?" the consultant asks.

"Really nailing down the questions."

"And?"

"I don't know."

"What don't you know?"

"Which questions to choose. Whether they're worded properly. Whether to go with a dozen or more like twenty. How I'm going to handle the responses."

"What do you think I'm going to say next?" asks the consultant.

"That instead of actually thinking about the work, I'm worrying about the work."

"Right. And?"

"That I should look at each question, quietly decide whether it's good or good enough or whether it should be discarded, and let the process unfold."

"Right. And?"

"And . . . to trust myself!"

Sam is entirely capable of evaluating his own work, but only if it's the work he's evaluating and not himself. He has yet to master his fear of evaluation: his fear that the work will reveal to anyone who glances at it that he is a fool and an impostor. He understands this intellectually, but it is still a terrible struggle to get this deep-seated fear quieted. For this project he may have to work with a consultant throughout, but even with a consultant's help it will be no easy matter for Sam to overcome this fear and produce work on a regular basis. It turns out that the last thing Sam wants to do is look in any mirror, funny or otherwise; this horror of mirrors is at the center of his difficulties.

Anne has been rushing right along on *Shooting Star*, her story of a young filmmaker collaborating with a world-famous director. At the halfway point a plot decision had to be made, whether to send her heroine off by herself or whether to have the director invite her to his estate, where his estranged wife also resides. Anne chose to send Celeste off by herself, but as soon as she did this a loud warning bell went off.

She decides to enter the funhouse. Many of the named mirrors provide her with information, but one does considerably more than that. When she holds her work up to the Mirror of Shape and Form she sees a startling image reflected—a broken branch, its broken half dangling down and almost severed off. She suddenly realizes that, all the good reasons to send Celeste off by herself notwithstanding, such a move is not legitimate in this book. She's broken some promise she can't even articulate by sending Celeste away; the image of the broken branch is proof. Seeing the broken branch convinces her that she must get Celeste to the estate and, more than that, she must make sure that something dramatic happens there. She commits to writing that scene and pledges to include in *Shooting Star* all the conflict and tension that popular fiction requires.

Henry has stopped having fun. Since he decided to write a memoir, he's felt blocked and unhappy. Some scenes have been fun to write, some have seemed on target, and some have surprised him by what they've revealed about his own motives. But more about the memoir has felt wrong than right. Bad headaches and the desire to drink have returned with a vengeance. Henry knows that something is wrong and that he must pause and take stock.

He goes out driving. Without aiming his car in any particular direction, he ends up at the beach. As he strolls along the sand, it comes to him that memoir is the wrong form for what he's attempting. It's a form that tempts him to lie too much, and it also tempts him to reveal too much about his sexual partners. Then what's the proper form? To know that he must know much more about his ideas and intentions than he presently does. Thoughts about bisexuality, addictions, mania, depression, the worlds of Hollywood and the New York theater, the state of America and the state of the human species are churning together like a stew on high boil. What does Henry want to say about all that? He just doesn't know yet.

Henry has been reading and thinking for eight months, but, as it turns out, eight months are not enough. He realizes that the answers and even the questions that deeply concern him are not presently known to him. That realization, rather than discouraging him, pleases him. He walks a little faster, with a new spring in his step. He is pleased at his own patience and pleased that he is operating with integrity. His seaside evaluation has led him to the proper conclusion: rather than leaping, he has much more looking to do. He sets himself the eloquent task of just continuing.

Breaking Your Heart, and Healing It

Every work must fall short in some sense or other. Even if we sometimes manage to produce a "perfect" book, we cry, "Why wasn't my other work this good? I'm such an idiot!" The Hindu monk Kirpal Venanji said, "Each time you judge yourself, you break your heart." Evaluating your work can lead to great satisfaction, when the work is strong, but there are always tears waiting to be shed, waiting for the moment when you look at the work from a new angle and cry, "There, that's where I failed it!"

These waiting tears scare us away from evaluating our work. We don't want the grief that our own evaluations can bring. But there is no real choice in the matter. It is one thing to know extremely little about a work as we sit down to write it. That is natural and proper. It is likewise natural, fair, and proper to have our first draft come out tangled and jumbled. But it is a very different thing to let that tangled jumble stand. Eventually we must face it and say, "Let me make some sense of this!" In our deep writing code of ethics, righteous evaluation is a prime commandment. Our hearts will mend, after all, as we take comfort in the knowledge that our work has been made better.

Doing
What's
Required

As a Zen monk once expressed it, great satisfaction lies as close as our next aware breath. Deep writers, when they can get out of their own way andachieve right silence, right intention, right relationship, and right effort, know that great satisfaction lies as close as the nearest slip of blank paper. Who would not want to experience a grave, ecstatic unlocking of the spirit of the word? Who would not want to write deeply?

We all want this. But much is required of us if we hope to craft true, beautiful things and get them to market. We are required to wrestle with our psychological demons. We are required to alter our self-talk so that we focus on our ideas and not on our frailties. We are required to intend to write, or else nothing will incubate. We are required to relate to our work and, when the time comes, relate to marketplace players. We are required to love our work and also to evaluate it. In the first six chapters I've described many of these requirements, and in this chapter I'll present several more.

One Fantastic Checklist

Everything on the following checklist is required if you're to write deeply. Following the list are descriptions of each requirement and exercises to help you meet them.

- ☐ I will relish ideas.
- ☐ I will capture ideas.
- ☐ I will get fit for the journey.
- ☐ I will orient toward my work.
- ☐ I will choose and commit.
- ☐ I will make incredible messes.
- ☐ I will enjoy the dangers of writing.
- ☐ I will honor the process.
- ☐ I will positively influence the process.
- ☐ I will write in the middle of everything.
- ☐ I will keep my work in mind.
- ☐ I will love and befriend my work.
- ☐ I will evaluate my work and make it right.
- ☐ I will keep fit for the journey.

1. I will relish ideas.

It is a love of ideas that motivates the deep writer. We all want to think more, to bring fresh excitement to our tired brain, to help it dream its dreams and make its deep connections. But to have these good things happen, we need to turn our attention and our intentions toward ideas. We need to orient ourselves toward ideas and make time for ideas.

Write a love letter to an idea. Let it know what you love about it, what you mean to do for it, and how you'd like to work with it to give it life. Ask it questions. Inquire about its health. Ask it what it needs and wants. Go to the post office and mail the letter to yourself. When the letter arrives, open it as eagerly as you would open a letter from a new lover. Read your love letter over. Isn't this the beginning of a fine affair?

2. I will capture ideas.

Toni Morrison said, "When I don't have a novelistic or narrative idea to fret, those are the bluest times." When an idea arrives, whether boldly, with trumpets blaring, or as unsure as a child visiting strangers, we must capture it so that the magic can begin. Once captured, elements of writing attach themselves to this frail idea like iron filings to a magnet. Language comes, plot comes, images come, opening sentences come. A new chaos is created out of which the order of a book can appear. But for this to happen, the frail idea must be grabbed out of thin air, where it dissipates if ignored.

Start an idea notebook. Fill it with anything you like: little line drawings, phrases, single words. "A raceless novel." "The history of green." "Utopia on an old boat." " 'Sensitive men.' " "A Coke can and a Pepsi can." "Throwaway people." "Public art." "Mania." "The daughter who got pregnant and disappeared." Enter into a special relationship with this idea notebook. In it, the first sparks of new work will ignite. Try to write something in your idea notebook every day.

3. I will get fit for the journey.

Becoming a deep writer means becoming a person who survives his depressions, breaks the hold of his freedom-reducing addictions, and maintains a fine solitude but also searches out intimacy. The deep writer manifests personality traits like passion, nonconformity, self-direction, empathy, and thoughtfulness—but, in the tradition of Goldilocks, neither excessively nor insufficiently. It is the work to become this sort of person—work on psychological strengthening and personality modulation—that prepares a writer for his writing journeys.

Create and practice a personalized set of "writer's coping skills." What will you include? Learning how to overcome shyness so that you can present your work comfortably to agents and editors? Doing your best to handle any inevitable depressions, maybe with the help of your writers' support group that meets every Wednesday? Figuring out how to heal the wounds of envy that keep you from loving the work of others? Learning anger management skills, anxiety management skills, boldness-building skills? Spend an afternoon in a sunny place with the idea of writer's coping skills and see what kind of list you generate.

4. I will orient toward my work.

The deep writer experiences a shift in consciousness away from the self and toward the work. This shift is permanent for as long as she is writing a particular piece, so that wherever she is and whatever she is doing—riding the bus or sautéing onions—she knows which direction to turn to recover her connection to her current work. You can tell from her body language and the look in her eyes that she is ready all the time, oriented toward her work even while doing the other things that life demands.

Tape a large piece of newsprint or butcher block paper on a wall.
Take off everything from the other three walls of the room, any
paintings, photos, or prints. Face one of the blank walls. This white-
ness is full of mysterious reality, but it is not where your writing is.
Turn and face the second wall. The fine cracks in the plaster are
mesmerizing, and you could create excellent tales out of them, but
you have other work to do. Turn and face the third blank wall. Yes,
the shadows are evocative and could make you cry, but they are for
another story and another time. Now turn and face the paper. This
is your current work and your current direction. Whenever you
want to feel a connection to your work, orient this way and feel the
work return.

5. I will choose and commit.

For the deep writer, each day starts with new choices and
new commitments. Yesterday you were working on a scene
between the bees and the spiders. Today you must decide if you
should return to that scene or let it percolate. Or maybe you
should turn to that other scene, the one between the raven and
the platypus. Between waking up and writing, choices like these
are incubating. Once made, they require a writer's pledge: that
she will really give the bees and the spiders, or the raven and the
platypus, her undivided attention.

If you have several new projects to choose from, write down each
of their names on separate slips of paper. Put each slip in a Ziploc
bag. If you're in the middle of a project, do the same, but fill the
bags with the names or numbers of your book's chapters. Put these
bags in the refrigerator, right on the top shelf where you can see
them. Each day, when you get out your bagel, cream cheese, and
milk for tea, take out the Ziploc bag that holds the name of that
day's work. Open the bag in a ritual way. Say something like "Today

is your day, Chapter 7." At the end of the day, put the bag away and say, "Good night, Chapter 7." Notice that the other chapters and projects are right there where you left them, nice and cool, available whenever you want them. Tomorrow you get to choose and commit anew.

6. I will make incredible messes.

Messes make work and invite punishment. If you make a mess in your kitchen, someone—probably you—will have to clean it up. When you made messes in childhood, probably you were rebuked or punished. These injunctions against making messes naturally carry over to our writing. The reasons not to make messes in our writing so outnumber the reasons to make them that, if we were counting, no writing would ever get done. But these reasons only outnumber their opposites: they do not outweigh them. The heavyweight reason to feel free to make enormous messes is that no creativity can occur unless we grant ourselves that freedom. All deep writing carries the risk that we will end up with forty-six thousand words of nonsense.

Buy a package of potato chips. Place a big chip on your kitchen counter. Raise your fist. Go ahead. Smash the chip to smithereens. Make a fine mess. If there are just too many good reasons not to make this mess, then this is exactly the mess you ought to be making. Get that chip royally smashed. As you clean up the mess, think about your writing. Aren't your fears gone? If some fear remains, get out another chip. Go to town on all the chips in your house.

7. I will enjoy the dangers of writing.

Why does writing feel so dangerous? Because our ego is on the line each time we commit words to paper. Our self-image is on the line. We are magnificent in criticizing others, but put a few words on the page and everyone gets to criticize us back.

Packs of wild dogs get to eat our words and spit them back at us. Am I overstating the case? I don't think so. Writing feels exactly this dangerous to most people. Are you secure enough to say, "Kick me, curse me, I will keep on writing!"? The dangers of a bruised ego and a lump on the heart never entirely go away.

Write with a tiger in the room. The tiger is sleeping right beside you, hardly three paces away. It may awaken at any time. When it does, it will be one hungry cat. You might be its next meal. Chat with this tiger telepathically so as to learn what each of its stirrings mean: which growl means nothing and which growl must be taken seriously. The room is filled with the smells of danger, but still it is possible to write. Can you do it?

8. I will honor the process.

Everything we do requires willpower and surrender. We exert our will to help influence the process, by demanding of ourselves that we write six days a week instead of two, by adding a month of revision time when we would like to be done already, by showing our work even though we are afraid of its reception. But we also surrender to the reality of process. Jupiter is too far to visit just by flapping our arms, and brilliance is too much to expect from every one of our syllables. We demand hard work from ourselves and surrender to the fact that only a percentage of the work will really please us.

Create a writing altar. Put up some pictures you draw of your future book covers and some sketches of readers entranced by your future books. In front of the pictures set out a fine pen and a cheap pen, an assortment of pencils, a special eraser, some blank note cards arranged like a fan. Hoist up the writing flag you've designed and sewn and sing your writing song (the one that you sing as you march to the computer). Give thanks that you are getting and making the chance to write. Vow to be a faithful servant of the writing process.

9. I will positively influence the process.

Imagine a plant growing in the wild. Now imagine the same plant being cultivated in a garden. In both cases the plant needs nitrogen, water, and its own special evolutionary luck, and who's to say that the wild plant might not grow strong and healthy in its accidental niche while the cultivated plant fails despite all our ministrations? Process is process, after all. Maybe you can write while drunk and turn out excellent things for a time (never mind that your life is otherwise in ruins). Maybe you can refuse to revise and still do fair work (never mind that your publisher has to hire a book doctor to get your bloated prose on a diet). But isn't it better to nurture the work? Isn't it better to cultivate your talent and help it grow, so that you actually do better over time and not worse? Isn't positively influencing the process a reasonable goal?

On a large erasable board, create a chart with two columns. Label one column "honoring the process" and the other "dishonoring the process." When you take a day off from writing, decide in which column to list that vacation. When you sleep late, enter that fact in one column or the other. When you discuss your work with a friend, drop one writing project in favor of another, or make a big plot change on the spur of the moment, figure out in which column each event goes. Use this chart to help you learn what you need to know about positively influencing the writing process.

10. I will write in the middle of everything.

In order to have ideas we need an available brain. If anything steals away our brain, it steals us away from writing. What steals the brain? Worries, first of all. Worrying about our coworker's promotion steals the brain. Worrying about the stock market steals the brain. Because we worry all the time about hundreds of small and large things, most of us do significantly less writing than we hope to do. We have two goals: to worry less, and to write even if we do have worries hovering about. The latter is a vital skill to learn, since life does not allow for all our worries to vanish.

Imagine that you are expecting a very important phone call: the results of a medical biopsy. Take your portable phone to the computer and boot the computer up. The phone may ring and the news may be terrible. Write anyway. Write when you are not thinking about the impending call, and write when the thought of it intrudes. Notice how the anxiety completely disappears sometimes, if only for a few minutes. Notice how you can write, unsteadily but bravely, even when the thought returns. Practice exercises like this one to learn how to manage your worries so you can write in the middle of everything.

11. I will keep my work in mind.

How do you remember that a pie is baking or that you need to pick your children up outside the skating rink at six? You might use a kitchen timer for the pie, but for the trip to the rink what most of us do is just *keep it in mind.* We keep scores of things in mind that we feel we need to remember. But too much of the time we don't keep our writing in mind, because it is not going well, say, or because the next plot twist is eluding us. In order to write, we must determine to remember that we have writing to do. Then we can go ahead and write.

Buy one of those portable music stands that marching band players wear to hold their music. Put some pages of your manuscript

into it. Then wear it. March around the house with pages of your
book right before your eyes. Do this every morning for five minutes
or right before dinner while the carrots are steaming. You can read
the pages as you walk and even revise them if you like, but the pri-
mary goal is to learn what everyday intimacy with your work feels
like.

12. I will love and befriend my work.

To write is to enter into a relationship with the self, with a
germinating idea, with language, with your work as it grows and
changes, with readers, with the world. If the ideal for each of us
as human beings is to be loving and compassionate toward others, the ideal for the deep writer is to bestow love, friendship,
and compassion on every piece of work he undertakes. Reality
usually falls short of this ideal, but by keeping the ideal in mind
the deep writer has a better chance of crafting a loving relationship with each new piece. It is better to feel silly loving your
own stories than to feel detached and indifferent.

Start a kindness journal in which you record your efforts at
friendship with your work. Imagine that it's time to show your work
to others. In your journal, discuss the specific things you intend to
do to help your work make the rounds of agents and editors. An
entry might read: "Personally, I enjoy dressing in Renaissance cos-
tume. But will my book feel comfortable arriving on an agent's
doorstep looking that odd and unconventional? Probably not.
Probably it would prefer to look neat and normal. So let me help
it. Let me put together a neat, normal-looking package. Let me tidy
its margins and buy it a nice mailer. That's friendship!"

13. I will evaluate my work and make it right.

Our goal is to create beautiful, powerful, insightful work.
To do this we have to be willing to examine our own work and

really see what we've written. We have to heed our own analysis and consider any analysis offered by readers, whose opinions may prove valuable. Then, almost certainly, we have revising to do. This revising may involve small changes, or it may involve revisioning and restructuring the whole book. All of this goes into making our work right.

When a phrase sets off warning bells, print it up very large, say, in

48 point type.

Paste it on the wall. Whenever you walk by it, give it some thought.

She came riding through the meadow on

her newly tamed palomino.

Is this where your historical romance should start? Or would it be better to begin it several days later, on the whaling ship as it puts to sea? You may love the sentence, but your job is to make order: what does the architecture of the work demand? Maybe your heroine must ride through the meadow on another day, in another novel.

14. I will keep fit for the journey.

Life tests us, and the writing life tests us doubly. You may drink herbal tea to ward off a cold, but what do you do to ward off an incipient writer's block? You may hire a massage therapist when your back gets knotted, but what do you do when your brain gets knotted over a plot tangle? You may do yoga to keep limber, jog to keep your heart healthy, and meditate to cleanse your mind. But what do you do to keep fit for the writing life?

Make up the following mental health mini-checklist in multiple copies, one for each day. Every day, before sitting down to write, check out your mental health.

☐ Am I depressed?
☐ Am I worried?

- ☐ Am I distracted?
- ☐ Am I manic?
- ☐ Am I sad?
- ☐ Am I in chaos?
- ☐ Am I unhappy with myself?
- ☐ Am I unhappy with something or somebody else?
- ☐ Am I unhappy with the writing?
- ☐ Have my addictions got the better of me?
- ☐ Has my anxiety got the better of me?
- ☐ Am I unequal to today's challenges?
- ☐ Am I in crisis?

Check off the statements that seriously apply to you. Then answer the following questions for each statement you've checked: (1) What will I do about this? and (2) Can I still find a way to write? In honor of each statement that doesn't apply, dance a jig of celebration!

Whose Job Is It?

A few weeks ago I spent an hour on the phone with an editor who works at a publishing firm specializing in books for psychotherapists. A year or two ago that house purchased a book from me based on a proposal. The editor who had purchased the book no longer worked there, and the editor with whom I was speaking made it clear that she would not have bought the book based on that proposal and that she could not see publishing the manuscript that I'd submitted, even though the manuscript had many good points and matched the proposal exactly.

In her opinion the existing manuscript had problems that would take more than cosmetic work to correct. She saw a good book in there somewhere, but whether that good book would ever emerge was an open question. She was returning the edited manuscript to me; the ball was in my court. She hoped that her news hadn't plunged me into despair.

It hadn't.

I had known all along that the book wasn't right. Part of me rejoiced in the editor's comments, because what she proposed constituted a second chance. The book would not be published in its present form, and I had a chance to redeem myself. Of course, I had plenty of reasons to want it published even in its weak form—to get the rest of the advance, to have another book out, to be done with it—but I had a better reason to be happy. I could celebrate that this book that wasn't right wouldn't get foisted on the world.

Why, then, had I submitted an inadequate proposal and, later on, an inadequate manuscript? For the reasons I just mentioned and for others exactly like them, having to do with not understanding the material at the outset, willingly fooling myself, and wanting the book published no matter what. There isn't a noble reason in the bunch, but these are among the common reasons why writers write less well than they can and should.

I'm sure all editors would agree that few of the manuscripts they receive are in good enough condition to be published. Rarely are they as good as the proposals or synopses that introduced them promised they would be. The author has said too little, or too much, or the wrong thing, or a different thing, or the right thing the wrong way. How did it happen that the author never understood what his book was about? Why did he include a whole chapter that had no reason for being? What blindness caused him to plot so poorly or to resolve the central conflict with a whimper?

Some of these things happened for unavoidable reasons, but some happened for avoidable reasons. The unavoidable ones are part of the process and can't be eliminated. But the avoidable mistakes are ours to try not to repeat. That is our job. That is the essence of what's required. Our job as writers is to learn more and to fool ourselves less. Our job is to work harder and to get our truths better shaped. Many of our messes are honorable messes, irredeemable but honest, and we have no reason to berate ourselves over them. Many of our worthy ideas will not make it into print, and many of our good books will not do well in the marketplace, and we can control only a small part of that. But there's the part that we can control: the love we can lavish, the sweat we can pour, the midnight oil we can burn, the honesty we can bring. I am only starting to learn this at age fifty-one. Thank God for the second half of life!

Good-bye, Hello

It is sad to say good-bye to our five writers. But we have one last snapshot to remember them by. Each has finished a manuscript. None could have predicted the shape their work would take when they first began hushing, holding the intention to write, and inviting in ideas. Nor can they say now that they see a clearly marked path to a published book. But each can feel proud about having done some real work.

Amelia completed her novel. Because of its setting in the

New York magazine world and because of its young female pro-
tagonists, it has a chance to interest publishing marketplace
players and readers. But because it is idiosyncratic, dark, personal, and literary, because it focuses as much on psychology as
on plot, and because it does not end happily, she is bound to
hear what sound like odd comments from agents and editors.
Many will comment that because her novel is "dark" or seems
"too quiet" it is unpublishable.

Amelia drafts a query letter, introducing herself and her
novel, and sends the letter out to five agents. Three do not
answer. A fourth writes her a brief, personal note saying that the
fiction market for first novels is a bear and that Amelia should
think about trying to publish in England. (That a novel set in
New York should need to be published in England is not an idea
that Amelia can get her mind around, but she shrugs and files
the letter away.) The fifth literary agent agrees to look at a synopsis and fifty pages.

Amelia has no synopsis to send; she spends several weeks not
writing one. She has no clear idea what the task is, and she balks
at the idea of trying to capture the essence of her work in a few
short pages. But finally she tries her hand at what feels like a
really odious task. She writes a synopsis, which turns out considerably less well than the novel itself, and sends it and fifty
pages off to the agent.

So begins Amelia's odyssey in the marketplace. She will do
many smart and many silly things and have many experiences,
most of them disappointing. One evening she'll chat with an
editor on-line. The following morning she'll brainstorm ways
of getting a chunk of her novel into a fashion magazine. Late
the next night, after two glasses of wine, she'll get on the phone

and tell her best friend that she intends to paint herself blue and streak the American Booksellers Association convention. Weeks and months will pass, and *Eggshell White* will not have sold to a publisher; but Amelia will be able to say that she is doing an honorable beginner's job of meeting the marketplace.

Marjorie, too, has completed her book. It has many flaws, which she can't yet identify because her closeness to the work has caused a case of writer's blindness. But if she goes ahead and markets the book and then returns to it in two or three months' time, with a fresh pair of eyes and some feedback from the world, she will begin to see that her plot is too convoluted, her chapter segues too casual, her minor characters too flat, and her detective a bit too unsympathetic. These are a lot of problems, verging on the uncorrectable. Still, she has written a whole mystery from beginning to end, revised it, loved it, hated it, sweated with it, and rejoiced in the goodness of some scenes. She too can feel proud.

But she doesn't. What she feels is scared. She is scared of what people—agents and editors, but really anyone—will say about her mystery. She is scared that, despite her education, intelligence, efforts, and everything else, she has made a fool of herself. So, instead of celebrating the completion of her first novel, she feels pain, a strange pain that feels worse than not writing ever did. It hurt not to write, but it hurts even more to have written something she fears is awful. It isn't awful, but she can't see that; she can't see it objectively at all. The manuscript is a burden and even a reproach, reproaching her for not being better, and so she puts it away, giving it a wide berth every time she passes the part of the study where it's kept.

She can't manage to call herself a writer, even though she has written a book. Instead of "writer" she thinks of herself as a novice writer, an unpublished writer, a middle-aged writer, an amateur writer, or worse. But Marjorie deserves to call herself a writer and to realize that books are written by people just like her. If there is any adjective she wants to attach to "writer," it should only be "deep." *The Old Lady Dies* is not perfect and not even good enough, but how much better could a revised draft of a first novel be? With luck, Marjorie will realize this and begin to show her novel in the world, taking the blows that come with showing and, when the time comes, finding the way to rework the book or start a new one.

Sam has managed to write his dissertation. He's gotten feedback, made necessary revisions, and had the dissertation accepted. He is thankful that this is all the writing he will ever have to do, that nothing along these lines will ever be required of him again. But a thought nags at him. He knows that writing the dissertation caused him to think about ideas and about life in a new way. Is he to stop thinking now? Is he to use his brain only in the service of company goals and savvy investing? How can he live a vital, meaningful life if that's all the thinking, creating, or meaning-making he ever gets to do?

Months back, Sam's creativity consultant suggested to Sam that he carve an article out of the dissertation and submit it to magazines. At the time, Sam pooh-poohed the idea. Now he wonders. An article feels almost manageable. He has the idea of engaging the consultant again and getting help on the article. He also thinks about attending an article-writing workshop. But all of a sudden he decides that he doesn't need help. Why can't he just write an article? He jots down a reminder to himself, one of the affirmations he began to use while writing the dissertation: "I respect my own efforts." The next day he starts on the piece.

Sam writes a small article based on his research. He has to rewrite it several times, but finally it feels complete. Then he doesn't send it out on submission. Maybe it really isn't good enough. And where should he send it? And who would want an article from him? After a painful month of not submitting the article it dawns on him that he's not sending it out because he's afraid. As soon as he says that to himself—as soon as he identifies his problem as fear—he feels liberated. What has he got to fear? Absolutely nothing! He sends the article out, not just to one place but to several. He doesn't think of himself as a writer, really, but he does feel like he's doing something brave and wise, something in support of his intention to use his talents and his mind.

Anne has written what can only be called a romance. Never in a million years would she have expected herself to tell the story she's told in *Shooting Star,* a story of innocence, optimism, sexual attraction, primitive conflict, and genuine good humor. But writing it has taught Anne a profound lesson. In a lifetime it is possible to write many books, including those one had no idea were dwelling within. In a lifetime it is possible to tell both dark stories and light stories, both hard truths and heartwarming fables. Anne understands that she has learned something important about versatility, flexibility, and truth-telling in a different voice. She also just flat-out likes her story.

Anne has done a remarkable job, writing a book that is both full-bodied and a quick read. Not only that, but writing it has actually changed her mind about life. Having given her main character vitality, enthusiasm, and a chance at love, she herself feels lighter and more optimistic. In fact, a week after she completes *Shooting Star,* she falls in love. This may sound like a fairy tale, but it isn't. For Anne, who has led the writer's life and lived in isolation, writing beautifully but suffering from nameless anxieties and severe depressions, this opening to lightness turns out to be a personal boon as well as a professional milestone. For her, *Shooting Star* is the epitome of the right project arising at the right moment.

Henry has gone on reading, writing, and honoring the process for almost a year, while working as a hired hand on screenplays to earn a living. Each of the ways he's framed his work has had to be abandoned. It didn't want to become a history of bisexuality in literature, a self-help guide for bisexuals, a memoir, or even a novel. It gave him a good feeling that he refused to pursue any of these projects too far down a blind alley, but that good feeling is gone now: all he has after a year are reams of notes and piles of book shards.

Then, one Saturday morning, Henry wakes up burning with an idea. He runs to the computer, sits down, and fires off a screenplay in seventy-two hours. It's the story of a young playwright whose play is coming to Broadway and who sleeps with virtually everyone in the production company—cast members, the director, light people, costumers, producers—in a manic, *Shampoo* kind of way. The screenplay ends with opening-night raves for the play and a last empty seduction for the distracted, unhappy playwright. The screenplay is a tragedy; or, if not a tragedy, then a cautionary tale, a truthful tale about out-of-control appetite.

Henry is torn between calling the screenplay *Broadway*

Perversion or *Opening Night.* He's also torn between ending it with that seduction scene or with a scene in which the playwright gets his comeuppance. That he can't decide between the two titles and two endings disturbs him and makes it that much harder for him to congratulate himself on his work. But he has done an excellent job. Filmgoers will leave the theater with a question on their lips: "Why in God's name are people built like that?" Henry hasn't answered that question for himself, but he's posed it honorably and beautifully in his new screenplay.

Maybe Amelia, Marjorie, Sam, Anne, and Henry will invite us to witness their forays into the marketplace in a future book of mine. I look forward to that, since these five deserve some publishing success. While the odds are long and the challenges grave, those odds can be shortened and the challenges can be met. Our five writers will need to learn some additional principles, make an effort to market as fervently as they wrote, hold new intentions, and become expert through hard knocks and real-world experiences. Then each may get to feel the profound satisfaction of seeing his or her deep writing in print or on the screen.

The Tenth Book

Benjamin Disraeli once remarked that only one out of ten books was worth publishing. He went on to conclude that "the greatest misfortune that ever befell man was the invention of the printing press." Like me, perhaps you don't see eye to eye with Disraeli on this matter, because you feel strongly about the worth of that tenth book. That tenth book is one of the best things human beings can produce. It is so valuable that we can tolerate the other nine books, even when they are multiplied by thousands and fill our bookstores to bursting.

I think that you mean to write that tenth book. It may not buy you a vacation house in Provence; it may not earn you much money at all. You will have to do other things to live, things to which you will have to pay attention. But the writing of that tenth book is a worthy task and a human-sized miracle. In it you bring ideas to life, ideas whose meaning and value you can't gauge until you wrestle with them in the writing. You'll sweat as you write that tenth book, you'll shed some tears, but once in a while you'll jump out of your chair, shivery and thrilled, when a sentence goes deep and comes out whole. You could go from birth to death and never experience anything finer.

Dear Reader,

I would love to hear your thoughts and feelings about this book, any of my other books, the writing process, and/or the writing life. If you're curious about the individual, group, or organizational work I do as a creativity consultant or about the workshops, lectures, and keynotes I give, you are also invited to get in touch.

Dr. Eric Maisel
P.O. Box 613
Concord, CA 94522-0613
E-mail: amaisel@sirius.com
Fax: (925) 689-0210
Phone: (925) 689-0210

About the Author

Eric Maisel is a psychotherapist and creativity consultant who works with creative and performing artists in his private practice and gives workshops for writers at writers' conferences and other venues. His twenty-two works of fiction and nonfiction include *A Life in the Arts, Affirmations for Artists, Fearless Creating,* and other books on the creative life. He teaches writing at St. Mary's College (Moraga, California) and holds a Ph.D. in counseling psychology, master's degrees in creative writing and counseling, and bachelor's degrees in psychology and philosophy. Dr. Maisel lives in Concord, California, with his wife, Ann Mathesius Maisel, and their two daughters, Natalya and Kira.